Learning to Disclose

PETER LANG
New York • Bern • Berlin
Brussels • Vienna • Oxford • Warsaw

Joni Schwartz and Rebecca Schwartz

Learning to Disclose

A Journey of Transracial Adoption

PETER LANG

New York • Bern • Berlin

Brussels • Vienna • Oxford • Warsaw

Library of Congress Control Number: 2020949334

Bibliographic information published by **Die Deutsche Nationalbibliothek**.
Die Deutsche Nationalbibliothek lists this publication in the "Deutsche
Nationalbibliografie"; detailed bibliographic data are available
on the Internet at http://dnb.d-nb.de/.

ISBN 978-1-4331-8395-9 (hardcover)
ISBN 978-1-4331-8392-8 (paperback)
ISBN 978-1-4331-8389-8 (ebook pdf)
ISBN 978-1-4331-8390-4 (epub)
ISBN 978-1-4331-8391-1 (mobi)
DOI 10.3726/b17538

For Matthew, Nathan, and Paul who journeyed with us.

CONTENTS

ILLUSTRATIONS

ACKNOWLEDGMENTS

Together, we want to acknowledge Rebecca's father, Paul, her brothers and Joni's sons, Nathan and Matthew as well as their wives Sarah and Sabrina. Although they may appear only sporadically in this book, their love, spirit, and soul are everywhere in who we are and who we have become.

To family members, who answered our queries about the Minnetonka chapter, Joni's sister and Rebecca's aunt, Elsie Machtemes and to Joni's brother and Rebecca's uncle, Denny Hlavacek who we asked to recall a few memories – thank you. To family members, Kathy Oliphant, Director of Teaching and Learning at Waconia Public Schools who provided background on education in Minnesota, and to Clark Machtemes, a Minnesota musician and artist, who gave us direction for research; you are both always willing to support and help; it means a lot. Thanks to the Excelsior Historical Society especially Steve Kobs who verified with archival materials W.E.B. Dubois's summer on Lake Minnetonka and directed us to playwright Kim Hines who wrote, *Summer in the Shadows*, about Dubois in Minnesota. Kim, thank you for taking the time to talk, answer questions, pick your brain, and read your writing; it made a difference both personally and in the writing.

The Czech chapter was aided by the insights and conversation with Mark Bruner, a career missionary to Slovakia and the Czech Republic and a dear friend. To our friends in Uganda, thank you, Irene, for taking such good care of us in Gulu. Your food, attention, kindness, and work made space for think-ing, feeling and writing. Kirunda Muzamiru the best safari guide in Uganda by far; your friendship and expertise mean the world to us. To Grace Amiya, your tailoring class at Gulu Women Prison is not only an act of love but a creative inspiration.

A special thanks to the original members of our Tuesday evening Restoration Writing Group in Bed Sty; John Proctor, Sylvester (Sonny) Jackson, Carolina Soto, Jackie Cangro, Marvin Wade, and Michael Colbert for giving us a community of writers to belong to. The 2018 National Endowment for the Humanities (NEH) Global Cities August Seminar at LaGuardia Community College, City University of New York: Tuli Chatterji, Sorin Cucu, Rondee Gaines, Anita Baksh, Rebecca Tally, Sonia Rodriguez, Olga Aksakalova, Allia Abdullah-Matta, Laura Tanenbaum, Nichole Shippen, Karen Miller, and Chris Schmidt read and gave us specific feedback early on. Your suggested readings and keen criticism was invaluable.

Cathy Powell without your editing and organizing skills this book would not be. You keep us in order. Thank you, dear friend. The cover design is by Emily Gallagher and Robert Pollock who embraced our story as we embraced them.

To friends and mentors who journeyed with Rebecca during critical tran-sitionary periods in Haiti, Congo and Uganda and continue to be strong moral and emotional support: Pierre and Carolyn Julien; Viviane Fils Aime; and Jiesha Perkins; Jen Silen, and Myonawai Artis, and Crystal Burrey.

Joni wants to thank Marvin Wade, Dario Pena, P. Harris and R. Watson who read chapters at the Queensboro Writing Group and made her believe that this story could have meaning across the human experience. Thanks to all the Queensboro Correctional Facility writing group members who carefully read drafts, gave encouragement, made suggestions, and embraced our stories.

To Joni's lifelong friends Sara Jorgensen Levy and Avril (Birdie) DeJesus who read chapters in the Bremen, Maine cabin in the woods in front of the fireplace and with a bottle of wine. The more we drank the better the man-uscript seemed. And to my dear friends, Damaris Miranda and Valerie Noel, who journeyed with us in the beginning; they know how to be a friend. To Andrea Emmanuel and Kurt Sealey for loving books and writing as I do and sharing this experience with me. Thank you, John Chaney, for your love, your support, your gentleness—for being there and being you—you are a great gift from God. And to our cat, History, who kept me company during copyediting.

ABBREVIATIONS

CHO	Christian Haitian Outreach orphanage
NGO	Non-governmental organization
CRT	Critical Race Theory

INTRODUCTION

This is soul work. A mother and daughter collaborative autoethnography engaging the social imagination and the emotional journey of learning to disclose. It is reflection on the places and histories that shaped us through transracial adoption.

If readers are looking for a memoir or a straightforward adoption story, this book is not it. Neither is it a research text on transracial adoption nor an autobiography. It is not a diary, a happy ever after story of how God worked in our lives, or a White savior story. And it is not the whole story.

Collaborative autoethnography analyzes personal experiences in the context of the surrounding culture. As collaborative autoethnography, *Learning to Disclose* is autobiographic, ethnographic, and interactive. Autoethnography is a critical research method with the "auto" meaning the self, "ethno" meaning culture, and "graphy" meaning writing; it uses personal experiences to critically examine sociohistorical grand narratives and discourses in which we find ourselves embedded. This is something that autobiography and memoir often does not do. We write dialogue using social imagination to understand our lives through the global, national, and local histories of the places and spaces we lived, worked, traveled, and called home. (Mills, 2000)

We don't pretend to be historians, but we recognize the power of place entrenched in complex histories and untold stories; and we tell how select places in the world speak to us, interact with us, live in us, and affect our relationship. Place is personal, and the personalities that constitute a place, speak (Deloria and Wildcat, 2001). We are convinced that history lives in the present: and as we present it in the chapters to follow, history is selective. The history we tell is not straightforward or chronological and may at times seem disparate, from healthcare in Austria, the ROMA in Czech Republic, to the Dakota Indians in Minnesota, and Shirley Chisholm. For some tastes the connections may be too loose; but the history is nuanced, and we hope uncovers the tensions and contradictions of transracial adoption. We tell our personal histories from our own positionalities; therein, these histories are not exhaustive or the only truth. They belong to others who were there, too, especially Rebecca's Dad, our brothers and sons, Nathan and Matthew, and many others.

As adults and co-authors, we explore our mother-daughter relationship through selective disclosure; therefore, major events and people who are dear to both of us are sometimes left out—they are stories for other days or stories that need to be left untold. We went where the journey took us.

Three Voices of Disclosure

We tell our narrative via three voices: the critical historical voice, Rebecca's voice and Joni's voice. The historical voice embodies both locations and people like Bedford-Stuyvesant, Lake Minnetonka, Port-au-Prince, and W.E.B. Dubois, Jean-Bertrand Aristide, and Shirley Chisholm. Then we intersect and interject our personal narratives and reflections with the critical history of these places and people. We excavate the past to see if and how we live these histories in the present.

We tell our lived experiences through this third historical voice perhaps in part to hide behind it. We are private people and disclosure and reflection is difficult, emotional work. However, this third voice is not only a crutch by which we veil our stories; it is also the scrim for framing them, a way we approach the labor of unmasking the past that lives in the present. To us, this approach seemed easier and more truthful. Sometimes our personal voices are monologues and at other times they are dialogue, and we switch back and forth from second person to third person during the dialogue sections. At times we directly address each other as if in conversation; at other times we speak separately. This may be jarring to readers, but it serves our need to at times distance ourselves. The voices are easily distinguished as they alternate between standard font and italics.

Chapter 1 begins with Rebecca's birthplace, Carrefour, Haiti juxtaposed with the birth of the Haitian nation and international adoption as the privilege of colonialism and White supremacy. We examine Flatlands, Brooklyn, the Orphan Trains and the early years of the adoption in Chapter 2, and then revert to an earlier time and Joni's birthplace in Minnetonka, Minnesota, where we grapple with colorism and Native American erasure in Chapter 3. Chapters 4 and 5 engage the Czech Republic and Vienna, Austria places that we spent time together for work, travel, and missionary projects. We return to Haiti in Chapter 6 as adults and as Americans intersecting the voice of Jean-Bertrand, Aristide and Liberation Theology. Focusing on Africa, in Chapters 7 and 8 we delve into the brutal histories of both Uganda and the Democratic Republic of the Congo including Idi Amin, Joseph Kony and the Belgium colonists as well as Rebecca's professional work in Uganda and the Congo. Chapter 9 returns to Brooklyn, Bedford Stuyvesant and gentrification and making our home in Brooklyn. Chapter 10 begins with the yellow dress that Rebecca wore leaving Haiti and concludes with a critical analysis of the Evangelical Adoption Movement in America. Ten chapters and three voices weave and capture the complexity and unconditional love and tragedy which is transracial adoption.

Our Process

Our autoethnographic data collection and analysis was like parallel play. Joni started writing in 1990 but as the years went on, it became clear to her that this was Rebecca's story too. Therefore, the book was put on hold for twenty-five years. As an adult, Rebecca was ready and willing to write. Our research began in earnest in 2015, and the project took steam when we published an article in the *Journal of Transformative Learning* entitled *Learning to Disclose: A Postcolonial Autoethnography of Transracial Adoption* in 2018. (Schwartz & Schwartz, 2018)

We collected data in Haiti, Brooklyn, and Uganda where we spent time together. Our method was to audio record our guided conversations then transcribe them for collaborative analysis. We drafted open ended interview questions prior to these taped conversations. In addition, we had consistent electronic and digital communication when apart. Data collection occurred over a four-year period, and we collected over 50 hours of conversations.

After transcribing the interviews and completing historical research, we did thematic coding for each chapter draft identifying themes that linked our relationship, adoption and the history of each location. Race and racism especially as it connects to transracial adoption emerged as central to our evolving mother and daughter relationship, and identity development. Interest convergence, cultural appropriation, transracial adoption as colonization, erasure, colorism, death, and faith were additional threads.. This was messy work as we communicated back and forth and did member checking while writing. We sent developing drafts through email, giving each other feedback, then revising and editing. We found our methodology more systematic over time.

We also found more ease with our process, each other, and the writing relationship as the months went on. We communicated more and more: face to face over food and travel, WhatsApp, email, phone conversations at all hours of the day and night and multiple time zones. We hit our stride in Rebecca's home in Uganda in 2019 where we spent a month together. Rebecca increasingly took ownership assuming responsibility for the research, analysis, and writing. As qualitative researchers making known your positionality is important, alerting the reader to your potential biases and the framework from which you see the world and your work. Our positionalities are from the perspective of a mother, daughter, social activist scholar, international human rights advocate, anti-racists, and Christians.

A Disclaimer

We are unapologetically Christians, but we are also critical of religion especially as it relates to the institution of adoption and racism. In some ways, we resonate with the young writer who often made the New York Times Bestseller list, thinker and mother, Rachel Held Evans who recently died at the age of 37. An article in *The Atlantic*, by Emma Green (2019), sums up much of what spoke to us about Evans:

> She was part of a vanguard of progressive Christian women who fought to change the way Christianity is taught and perceived in the US ... The lasting legacy of Evans's writing, and of her public life, is her unwillingness to cede ownership of Christianity

to its traditional conservative male stewards --- her unwillingness to give up on Christianity, period ... Her very public, vulnerable exploration of a faith forged in doubt empowered a ragtag band of writers, pastors, and teachers to claim their rightful place as Christians.(p.1)

We have not given up on Christianity either, despite our critical stance on its' historical and contemporary ills. Instead we reclaim it, and reframe from a liberationist, social justice and monastic lens as we forge our faiths and tell our stories. And as Held Evans so aptly said about God, Jesus and storytelling,

> Jesus invites us into a story that is bigger than ourselves, bigger than our culture, bigger even than our imaginations, and yet we get to tell that story with the scandalous particularity of our particular moment and place in time. We are storytelling creatures because we are fashioned in the image of a storytelling God. May we never neglect the gift of that. May we never lose our love for telling the tale (2018, p. 72).

And like, Held, we in no way wish to tarnish our faith, so we attempt to speak our truths with vulnerability and humility.

Vulnerability

Zora Neale Hurston (1942) wrote, "There is no agony like bearing an untold story inside you." In this book, we try to muster the courage to show up and bring our untold stories out so they can be heard. In a time when social media makes disclosing free and easy, we do not feel so. We find disclosing hard work, begging for boundaries and privacy. Yet and still, we write albeit with sometimes great difficulty. Said (1996) stated after writing,

> I say and write these things because after much reflection they are what I believe; and I also want to persuade others of this view. There is a complicated mix between the private and the public worlds, my own history, values, writings and positions as they derive from my experiences, on the one hand, and, on the other hand, how these enter into the social world where people debate and make decisions about war and freedom and justice. There is no such thing as a private intellectual, since the moment you set down words and then publish them you have entered the public world (2016, p. 12).

And so, it is with *Learning to Disclose* we enter the public world; we hope with equal portions of critical reflection, humor, social imagination, and racial humility—and yes, vulnerability.

References

Deloria, V. and Wildcat, D. (2001), *Power and place*. Golden, CO: Fulcrum Publishing.

Green, E. (2019, May 6), Rachel Held Evans, Hero to Christian Misfits. *The Atlantic*. https://www.theatlantic.com/politics/archive/2019/05/rachel-held-evans-death-progressive-christianity/588784/ Accessed August 7, 2019.

Held Evans, R. (2018), *Inspired: Slaying giants, walking on water, and loving the Bible again*. Nashville, TN: Nelson Books.

Hurston, Z. N. (1942). *Dust tracks on the Road*. New York: Random House.

Mills, C.W. (2000), *The sociological imagination*. New York: Oxford University Press.

Said, E. (1996). *Representations of the intellectual: The 1993 Reith Lectures*. New York: Vintage Books.

Schwartz, J. & Schwartz, R. (2018). Learning to disclose: A postcolonial autoethnography of transracial adoption. *Journal of Transformative Education*. 16(1), 39–57.

· 1 ·

CARREFOUR, HAITI

"One must learn disclosure."

Stephen Brookfield

Adoption is a curious sort of birthing, but birthing, nonetheless. The labor is as intense as physical birth, but it is of a different variety. There is the waiting, the anxiety, insecurities, the fear of inadequacy; but there is also the exquisite joy of seeing and holding the new family member. Outsiders frequently hold distorted perceptions of adoption especially transracial adoption as though you do not love the same because you are not *really* mother and daughter; in other words, you did not give physical birth. But outsiders cannot know, cannot be expected to know.

To talk authentically about transracial adoption, it seems to us that living the experience, being present in the relationship matters. We are in a relationship of transracial adoption; we have been there, and we are there—that matters. And context matters also, the politics, the economics, the social structure, the culture and language, and of course the history. Each adoption has a story and a counter story, beginning in the history of the adoptee's country of origin. Adoptions from what have been erroneously called "third world" countries do not happen in a vacuum nor do they occur because parents do no love or want to raise their children; they happen because of poverty, complicated histories, and sometimes exploitation.

The Orphanage, Carrefour

It was November 6, 1980 and we were told that Rebecca was born in a hospital and her birth mother died in childbirth. Later there would be no way of knowing if that was accurate or not. The chaotic record-keeping, or lack of record-keeping, of the Haitian government would make tracking lineage impossible. On Rebecca's birth certificate would be the name of the mayor of Port-au-Prince as the father; thousands of children had his name on their birth certificates—they were wards of the state. Rebecca was transported to Christian Haitian Outreach (CHO) Orphanage as a newborn and would spend the next nine and a half years there. CHO is located outside of Port-au-Prince, off the Carrefour Road in an extremely poor section of the country. In the 1970s and into the 1980s, Carrefour was teaming with tourism, both foreign and domestic; but after the fall of the Duvalier regime and the country's instability, the tourism industry all but collapsed. Around this time, an American missionary Eleanor "Mom" Workman found CHO in Carrefour;

Figure 1.1   Christian Haitian Outreach orphanage (CHO). Source: https://christianhaitianoutreach.org/

this would be the place where Joni and Paul Schwartz, a Caucasian couple from New York, would meet Rebecca and adopt her in October of 1990.

Birthing of a Nation

Disturbingly displayed in a recent U.S. Presidential dialogue was the comment about Haiti being a "shithole" country. These perceptions of Haiti abound: the poorest country in the Western Hemisphere; a voodoo nation; culturally resistant to progress; a population of victims; a country with little connection, marginalized from the post-modern West. History however tells a different story. Haiti has been intertwined with that of Europe and the US for three centuries, and today's Haiti cannot be understood without an understanding of its complex both rich and tragic history (Dubois, 2012).

Haiti was born out of a tortuous and unjust world on an island that may have been one of the richest, beautiful and most productive in the 1700s Pearl of the Antilles (Dubois, 2012). It was then known as Saint-Domingue, a French colony made up of enormously profitable yet horrific slave plantations. These sugarcane and coffee plantations were worked by roughly a million imported African slaves who consistently died premature deaths due to the brutal nature of the environment plantations. The produce was exported to European consumers, making the French plantation owners exceedingly rich (Dubois, 2012).

It was into this context that Haiti was born. Beginning in 1791, slaves revolted on the plantations of northern Haiti and within two years established freedom for all plantation slaves. A former slave and French general, Toussaint Louverture, defended the new Haiti from further European invasion and made way for the establishment of a formal declaration of independence.

In a time of colonization and slavery, the world was not ready to support this first Black sovereign nation led by former slaves. It was a threat to the institutions of slavery, White supremacy, colonialization in France, Europe overall, and the US. Haiti's subsequent enforced political and economic isolation combined with European and American unwillingness to recognize the first Black nation would have ramifications for centuries to come (Katz, 2013).

Race, Postcolonialism and Transracial Adoption

This history also had ramifications for the institution of adoption, and how we understand ourselves and our racial identity within our mother and daughter relationship. Delgado and Stefancic's (2012) Critical Race Theory (CRT) says that race is endemic to America and our world—we cannot avoid it. It is embedded in our national sin of slavery and ongoing oppression of people of color as it is institutionalized. CRT understands race to have no bases in biology and in that respect is not real, but it is socially constructed and therefore real in its consequences (Duster, 2001). Real in its consequences like the phenomena of mass incarceration, inequality in educational access and healthcare, segregation in real estate and even present in the institutionalization of adoption through policy and privilege. Adoption is a seemingly altruistic practice and adoptions of poor children from the colonized worlds inextricably connect colonialization and race. Haiti's colonial history is no different.

"Haiti was postcolonial before postcolonial was cool" (Curtis, 2014). Simply understood, postcolonialism is the period following colonialization; existence following a nation becoming independent from colonial rule. From this perspective, Haiti has been in an uneasy postcolonial period far longer than other former colonies. By the first half of the 20th century, the worldwide colonial project of European empires reached perhaps their greatest advance. Many non-European peoples and nations were conquered and occupied. This was when the first ideas and narratives around transracial adoption developed (Hubinette, 2006; Wexler, 2000).

Hubinette, a researcher and a political activist interested in issues of adoption and racism especially as it focuses on the adoption community of Korea, describes the origins of transnational and transracial adoptions as "forced child migration" and "the trafficking of an estimated half a million children to date" (Hubinette, 2006, p.1).

Hubinette (2006) uses gender studies scholar, Laura Wexler's (2000) term *imperial sentimental narrative*—a narrative of reparations, reconciliation, and salvation to explain the development thinking around the adoption of non-White children by European upper-class families. Hubinette goes on to say that these early *sentimental narratives* predated the real beginnings of transracial and transnational adoptions in the 1950—70s during a time of decolonization during the Cold War (Eske, 2010). Perhaps the most noted adoption work was that of the Holt family in the 1950s to help Amerasian children orphaned after the Korean War. This Christian motivated movement became Holt International, Inc. and is still involved in international adoptions today (Univ. of Oregon, 2012; Gravatar21, 2011; Dewan, S., 2000).

In the 1950s, transracial adoption was initiated as a rescue mission with strong Christian fundamentalist, particularly Lutheran undertones.

Subsequently, it came to be perceived as a progressive act of solidarity during the left, liberal 1960s and 1970s. Since the 1980s and continuing through today, international adoption has developed into the consumerist choice in the leading adopting countries and regions of the US and Scandinavia (Hubinette, 2006).

Regarding the suggestions that international adoptions, including Holt International Children's Services adoptions, could be characterized as a type of child trafficking or forced migration; Margaret Patterson an adoptive mother and adult education researcher responded:

> He (Hubinette, 2006) could not be more wrong . . . While I have no doubt that some individuals and even agencies do traffic children, Holt International is not one of them. In Korea, according to Bertha Holt who I met before her passing, the biracial children of Korean nationals and US soldiers were summarily rejected and frequently left to die (M. Patterson, personal communication, April, 2015).

Patterson goes on to clarify Holt International adoptions as one of the largest and most successful international adoption agencies that cannot be characterized and is the furthest thing from a "consumerist choice, child migration or trafficking."

Our Birthing Story

Rebecca

I don't like going back to that place—the orphanage—in my memory. I guess because I didn't feel safe there although often, I was very happy. I was a child and there was so much I did not understand. One memory that stands out was when my friend, Bernadette, said there was a man from the neighborhood working at the orphanage who would give you a gourde if you let him touch your private parts. Then you could buy a coke or candy which was a major treat. Bernadette did and I am not even sure what I did. We sure did like soda pop and candy.

Joni

I remember the Carrefour Road, the biggest bottleneck in Haiti. It is a two-lane pothole filled, dirt road which connects Port-au-Prince to Carrefour, which is only four miles away. But this road, also known as Route Nationale #2 is so full of traf-fic—taps-taps, pyeton, machan fresco, kawotchouman, chofe lanfe, kamyon dlo, kamyon baskil and every other vehicle trying to move from Carrefour to Port-au-Prince. I remember my second trip to Haiti, arriving to adopt you at the airport in 1990 and your little skinny body making its way through the crowd to me, looking up at me and latching yourself onto my arm and waist for the next few days so that I would not return to the US without you—riding the Carrefour Road with a nine year old pressed up against my sweating body, holding on for dear life.

Rebecca

All of us wanted parents. We would pray for parents. Somehow, we knew that being in this orphanage, even though it was all we knew, was not the way it was supposed

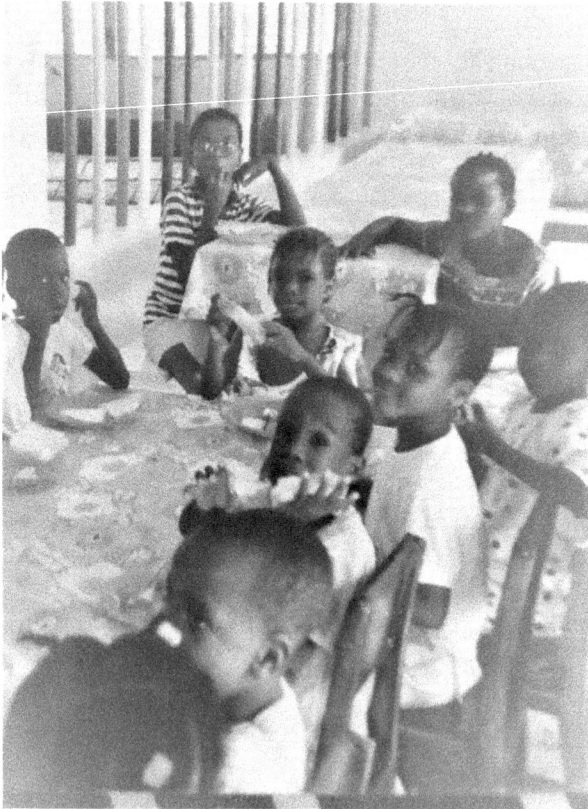

Figure 1.2   Rebecca at CHO before adoption. Source: https://christianhaitianoutreach.org/

to be. There were a few times when I was supposed to be adopted, but I was always disappointed. It wasn't until I was eight, almost nine that my parents, you, took me to America. By then I was used to defending myself, and I was guarded and careful about getting close to anyone especially you, Dad and two White brothers, Nathan and Matthew.

Joni

We arrived the first time at the Carrefour orphanage to find a baby girl. We already had two sons by birth; Nathan who was seven years old and Matthew who was three years old and now we wanted a girl. Arriving tired and hot from a tap tap ride from the airport, we saw what seemed like hundreds of boys between the ages of three and fifteen, jumping and shouting and trying to put their arms around us saying in Creole "adopt me", "be my mommy and daddy."

Transracial Adoption as White Privilege

For Tobias Hubinette, Korean adoptee and adoption scholar, international adoptions which are frequently transracial are the privilege of Whites; thus, in a postcolonial world the extension of colonial privilege and hegemony. He cites both the orphan train (Holt, 1992) where the non-White adoptive parents were forbidden to adopt White children and in pre-Civil Rights America, a handful of states even went so far as to legislate against interracial adoption or even the fostering of White children by non-Whites. In the late 1990s a widely publicized controversy erupted, when a Black woman in Detroit wanted to adopt a White girl. (Kennedy, 2003).

In 1972, The National Association of Black Social Workers (NASBW) expressed strong reservations against the practice of transracial adoption for the following reasons: White families could not support their Black children in navigating a racist society, White parents would not impart a strong sense of Black identity and self- worth, and White families would separate Black children from and prevent them from integrating with the Black community. The NASBW stated that at best, transracial adoption is ill advised; and at worst, it is a form of ethnic genocide (NASBW, 1972). Since 1972, the NASBW has stepped back from this position; nevertheless, it still remains a strongly held view that transracial adoption should be a choice of last resort when other avenues for same-race adoptions have been exhausted (Bartholet, 1991; NASBW, 2003).

Despite this history, most adoption research takes on a more balanced perspective as exemplified in the work of Smith, D., Cardell, J. and Juarez, B., 2011. Smith writes his ongoing blog about race and adoption from an American vantage point.

> Although I strongly understand their viewpoint and agree whole-heartedly with the NABSW rationale, I also believe that White adopting parents have every good intention in raising their children with love. The reality is that the majority of Black children in foster care will stay there until they age out on their eighteenth birthday, and I certainly cannot say that this is a better alternative to being reared in an all-White context. However, I believe there is an additional alternative, and that is to encourage White parents to educate themselves and take ownership of their place in history and the unearned benefits they receive from a racist society (Smith, 2012).

Specifically, for Haiti, the 2010 earthquake brought the complicated institution of transracial adoption which traditionally and predominantly involved White parents from Canada and the US into the forefront. Corruption, in the form of child trafficking and the compassion of adoption were both manifested. According to Reitz, through the department of Homeland Security, the Special Humanitarian Parole for Haitian Orphans short- term program was developed to expedite legal, legitimate adoptions already in progress or near finalization when the earthquake hit (Reitz, 2010; U.S. Citizenship and Immigration Services-USCIS, 2010). Through this program, an estimated 1200 Haitian orphans were approved to travel and be adopted through an expedited process immediately following the earthquake; the program was open for a specified time period and then closed by request of the Haitian government and normal international adoption processes restored (USCIS, 2010). Reitz and other adoption specialists, view international adoption and transracial adoption from a very different framework:

> Intercountry adoption is a form of immigration. It is offering some of the most vulnerable—orphaned or abandoned children—a permanent home and the chance to become one of us. Adoption in any form is an incredible act of generosity and kindness . . . There is no better or worse, no right or wrong, in offering a homeless child a home and a chance . . . (Reitz, 2010, p.792).

Post colonialist theorists take a divergent view encapsulated in Hubinette and Arvanitakes's (2012) quote about what they call the "glorification of today's White adopters of third world children."

> . . . interracial families and transracial adoptions of our time seek to complete the processes of conceptualized autochtonisation, [indigenization] thereby encapsulating the

desire to live with and become the *Other* in a way that had not been accomplished previously. Here we see the division between the Western *Self* and the non-Western *Other* collapse into an antiracist transracial fantasy of postcolonial reconciliation, White cosmopolitanism and a vision of a future global family . . . White people can finally feel that they are comfortable with non-White people and at home in the non-Western world. (p. 703)

Patterson has taken argument with Hubinette and Arvanitakes's (2012) terminology of "glorification" and "fantasy of postcolonial reconciliation", stating:

What if the adoptive parents *aren't* glorified? Some people have praised us for taking an orphan from overseas, stating how "good" we were and what a "blessing" it was for our daughter to have us. We had to reply that we were the ones who were blessed by her coming into our family. Other people have been highly critical . . . constantly being noticed for our decision, or having to explain the relationship to strangers, doesn't feel much like glorification!

Patterson goes on to say,

It is an interesting word choice, this "fantasy." When you are up with a sick child in the night who is howling because she has an ear infection, or sitting with her as she struggles line by line through a difficult homework assignment, there is no fantasy, only harsh reality, that of a child who needs her parent (M. Patterson, personal communication, April, 2015).

Much scholarly research has been done in the field of transracial and international adoption over decades and there are multiple and complex findings as well as multiple political positions taken on this emotionally and historically charged issue (Chuang, 2010; Patton, 2000; Kirton, 2000; Simon, Alstein, Melli, 1994). Certainly, the emotion-laden arguments and historical context previously presented raise tensions in our understanding of our own relationship with the sometimes-resultant feelings of guilt and shame. It is into this dialogue, tension, and diverging views that we situate our autoethnography.

Dialogue and Disclosure

Rebecca

"I think we are all over the place. It all seems so disjointed and coming from different angles." I told this to my mother after reading over one of our first drafts of this chapter. How do you relate history, to us, to adoption? I had never thought about all

of the different perspectives on transracial adoption and colonialism, but I guess it all makes sense. How can you argue with history?

For me though, I don't want to go back. The past is the past, and there is nothing I can do to change it. I feel I must look forward. So why have I agreed to write this with my mom? For she is my mom. Sometimes even as an adult I call her "mommy." We are very close. I feel this is the way my life was supposed to be. I do want to work on this project with her, knowing that she is more engaged in this autoethnography than I am, because I am preoccupied and sometimes a little overwhelmed with my job at the NGO and being back in Haiti. At the time I am writing this chapter, I have returned as an adult to work in my country of birth.

Creole is coming back to me. I stopped speaking it when I was adopted on October 11, 1990, my dad's birthday and my adoption birthday. I seldom disclose about my adoption; I am very private. I was nine almost ten years old, and in 1990 Haiti was going through major political, economic, and social turmoil following the Duvalier regimes and under the provisional government of Ms. Ertha Pascal-Troullot who took office in March of 1990 with the intention of ushering in free and fair democratic elections. President, Jean-Bertrand Aristide would be elected in December of 1990, two months after I left. I suspect that this "window" of time aided the ability of my parents to adopt and "get me out" of Haiti. Leaving the turmoil of Haiti, I entered my own tumultuous journey in America.

I grew up in an American orphanage in Carrefour founded and developed by an African American missionary named Eleanor "Mom" Workman. As children, we were almost never allowed outside the walls of the orphanage compound which was sort of a walled fortress where we lived and went to school and church. Although I was fluent in Creole and had been taught French, I was nearly fluent in English as well. Many of the volunteers and workers were American or Canadian, and because I had a good ear, I learned English from the American missionaries. In some sense, we were little Americans within the orphanage seeing very little of Haiti. I guess this was for our protection.

I prayed to God to be adopted. I guess I never was specific with God, not asking for Black or White parents, so my parents and two brothers are White. I never questioned my parent's motives, and I never looked back until now. I was told my birthmother died in childbirth. I was also told that I was on a government list to be sent to France—a child trafficking list—to be transported for child pornography and child prostitution. It is all so mixed up, just as Haiti is mixed up. But I am proud of being Haitian. Haitians are resilient and so am I. I am a survivor and a fighter like Haiti. I am proud of my people—their resilience and their fighting spirit.

Figure 1.3 Eleanor "Mom" Workman – founder CHO. Source: https://christianhaitianout reach.org/

Joni

I understand that in Caribbean culture and many cultures outside of American White culture, you can call many people your mother. But I don't like it when other women, well-meaning women mostly Black, call Rebecca their daughter or their adopted daughter. I guess I am sensitive. I admit it. I am Rebecca's mother—they can be her Auntie or Aunt—but I am her mother. When Rebecca says that it is all "mixed up" and being a fighter, I resonate with both those feelings. The past few years my reading and studying of Haitian history and transracial adoption has presented a disorienting dilemma. I now more than ever admire the bravery of the Haitian people and detest the continued well-meaning undermining of the Haitian government, economy, and the ability of the Haitian people to succeed as the first Black republic. I understand how some scholars understand transracial and international adoption to be just another colonialistic tool of predominantly White Europe, America and Canada. How do I make sense of this in my relationship with my daughter? For she is my daughter, not my adoptive daughter.

Like my daughter, I think I am a fighter. I have fought to be her mother despite my own insecurities and perhaps the perceptions of others. In the days before my mother, Rebecca's grandmother, died we found her napping in the fetal position and now I somehow sense that going back to birthing is a way of understanding both the life process and our steady progression to death. So for me, this whole journey of going back to so many births: the birth of Haiti, Rebecca's birth and birthplace, and adoption as a birthing is perhaps a journey to the death of old ideas and the birth of new ways of knowing and understanding my relationship with my daughter as an adult child.

Rebecca and I were with my mother, my daughter's grandmother in the hours and days before she died. In the emergency room, we were the first to hear the words from the doctor "she is trying to die." We stood by her side expressing how we loved her, talking to her, singing, crying. Two adults—mother and daughter—these stories are all sort of mixed up in my mind—the true stories of my mother's death, Haiti's birth and many deaths, Rebecca's birthplace and adoption, and the birthing and growing of our relationship. Perhaps my daughter is exactly right when she said, "I think we are all over the place. It all seems so disjointed and coming from different angles." And yet, I want to fight to tell the story of adopting my child, my Black child. Pearl Buck wrote about this experience in this way and I resonate with her experience:

> Adopting a Black child into my White family has taught me much I could not otherwise have known. Although I have many Black friends and read many books by Black writers, I rejoice that I have had the deep experience of being mother to a Black child. (1972, p.64)

Rebecca

Returning to Haiti has been and continues to be transformative for me. I lead a group of worshippers during church and Bible study services on a regular basis. Our team of singers consists of all Haitian natives, and we sing and worship in Creole. The sounds, language, rhythm and tone of both the music and Creole stir me and engage me in the music in a way that English does not. It is this return in my soul that is significant and transforming at several levels.

When I first arrived in Haiti to work, now almost two years ago, I used to close my eyes in the van as we drove through the streets. Perhaps I was not used to the poverty and pain of my Haitian people and found the realization disorienting. This idea of a disorienting dilemma rings true. As an adult returning to Haiti, I understand that I was fortunate to be adopted by my parents, and I told them that I was thankful. Verbally this was new, and I think this verbal declaration has made our relationship even stronger, I am still learning, still trying to make sense of it all.

Joni

To my shame, I did not start investigating Haitian history until several years ago when Rebecca was in graduate school studying international relations. Since the inception of this writing, I have immersed myself in the history and literature of Haiti and intend to continue to do so. This is transformative learning for me both in my recognition that because I have White privilege I could afford to know very little about my child's cultural heritage and history; from a position of privilege, I could afford to have that all be invisible including the aspects of Haitian history that suggest the collusion of America and Europe in the oppression and continued oppression of Haiti to this day. From this postcolonial perspective, I am forced into a disorienting dilemma and a painful recognition—the first step in Mesirow's transformative learning stages (Mesirow, 2009). The self-examination of this feeling of shame of somehow being unknowingly a part of an intrinsically oppressive institutionalized structure is the painful part and yet experiencing such a deep mother-daughter bond is shameless.

Along with other scholarly work that I have engaged in, this critical self-examination has led me to assume the role and to label myself as both a social activist scholar and anti-racist ally. Transformative learning theory states that in this kind of adult learning, which really is the core or should be the core of all adult learning, you not only assume new roles in light of new knowledge but then develop competence and confidence in those roles. The result is the integration of the new learning into your identity, relationships, work, and entire life. This can certainly describe the process of having been and continuing to engage in this research.

In terms of my relationship with my daughter, it has matured me and made me more confident of my role as her adult mother and her friend. I am not totally conscious of how this occurred. But I do know that understanding the history of her country of origin and brave heritage has made me even more proud of her and her contribution to our family. I have a renewed respect for my daughter, her current work and her cultural heritage. Perhaps it has helped me to relate to her as an adult and not as the little child we adopted. At some level, I feel a deep affinity for Haiti, through my daughter, a deep connection to their ongoing struggle for independence and social justice.

Rebecca

I do feel an affinity to the Haitian people, my people, but I am also an American because of my adoption. So, as an American, I was forced to confront race. Yes,

I think I can say this study has contributed to my learning, awareness and personal struggle with my racial identity. I was colorblind growing up; we as a family were colorblind. My adoptive parents never talked about race much therefore I never saw myself in a racial way; I just saw humanity. But as an adult, things are changing not just because of this study, but I will say that this study does push opportunities to talk about what we seldom spoke about but was always present—race. So now I am aware and now I cannot go back to colorblindness. And it is like I am making myself look in the mirror as I come to this consciousness, that there is color and I am Black, and what am I going to do with this?

Joni

I think I regret not discussing and grappling with race earlier in our relationship. I guess we were so busy bonding as child and mother, and I had not yet articulated my own racial identity. From my position of privilege, I did not have to recognize that I was White—in fact, this racial recognition did not come until much later in life. Embracing my White racial identity perhaps made me feel that I might be more distant from my daughter and all I wanted was to be close—to bond as mother and daughter.

Rebecca

I don't know if I will ever come to terms with it—racial identity. It is very complex for both of us, this learning. Through this awareness of Haiti's history and colonialism, I am forced to see the injustices. What kind of a system creates orphans like me? A system where a biological mother cannot raise her child? I never saw the world that way before.

But from that history and system came another system (international adoption) where my White mother can still raise a Black child; the mother-daughter relationship is colorblind in my mind. And it has produced positive agency. By that I mean that transracial adoption, despite its history and perhaps colonialist undertones, is a positive experience. Look at the outcome. Look at the person it created and is still to be finished. For example, it is weird for me to see people only having Black friends, or White friends, for that matter. I deal easily with different people; I am comfortable in international, intercultural and interracial settings. The world needs people like me.

Joni

My daughter said that she wanted to make sure that we communicated that all is not negative and that with transracial adoption there is, in her words, a "ray or glimmer of hope and a positive outcome." I agree for so many reasons, among them for me comes this awareness and better understanding of my racial identity and learning to be a mother to an adult child.

Rebecca

Maybe the transformational learning is in the personal struggle, the awareness of our racial identity. It seems race is a contentious topic in this current time; it is important to understand it within the context of our relationship from the perspective of history. I think we have a contribution to make to others—our relationship and how we make sense of it is a prototype of sorts, I believe.

Don't Push the River

Returning to Brookfield's opening quote "One must learn disclosure" (2011), we add our own quote gleaned from our ongoing transformative and reflective process- "Don't push the river" which comes from an old Chinese proverb. For us learning and choosing to disclose are transformative but in choosing we cannot hurry or "push" the process. It came at a pace comfortable and acceptable to us. "We do not want to push the river" as we are exploring deeply painful and strong emotions and memories, and this cannot be forced or rushed. This means that our autoethnographic research has been slow, deliberate, intentional, rigorous, and methodical and the telling of our counter story interwoven with the complexities of history, racism, colonialism and geography—for us these complexities live in the present moment with us and within our relationship.

Joni

Coming to terms with our racial identity is at the core of what we have learned so far. And indeed, there has been some transformation in our relationship; for me as a White mother of a Black adult daughter—I am both more and less comfortable "in my skin." More because I know she loves me despite my Whiteness and less because I understand more deeply the systems and institutions that made us mother and daughter.

Rebecca

I can no longer be colorblind. I am forced to grapple with being Black, understanding what that means to me and others in a racialized world. How do I take ownership of what is happening to me now? And how do I communicate that there is hope and agency in my relationship with my mother and White family despite the evil systems of colonization that seemingly led to these relationships? How can I live in this world as a model or prototype—because that is what I would like to be for others also struggling with their racial identity, like me, so that they can know they can be border crossers—across race and nationality? Some questions are not yet answered. The river continues to flow.

References

Bartholet, E. (1991). *Where do Black children belong? The Politics of Race Matching in Adoption,* 139 U.Pa.L.Rev. 1163.

Brookfield, S. (2011). When the Black dog barks: An autoethnography of adult learning in and on clinical depression. In T.S. Rocco (Ed.), *Challenging ableism, understanding disability, including adults with disabilities in workplaces and learning spaces: New directions for adult and continuing education* (132, pp. 35–42). San Francisco, CA: Jossey-Bass.

Buck, P. (1972). I Am the Better woman for having my two Black children, *Today's Health,* p. 64.

Chuang, A. (2010, Feb. 9). Haiti's orphans and the transracial adoption dilemma. Retrieved: http://www.theroot.com/articles/politics/2010/02/haitis_orphans_and_the_transracial_adoption_dilemma.3.html. Access date March 10, 2010.

Delgado, R. & Stefancic, J. (2012). *Critical race theory: An introduction.* New York: New York University Press.

Dewan, S. (2000, August 2). Bertha Holt, 96, a leader in international adoptions. *New York Times.* http://www.nytimes.com/2000/08/02/us/bertha-holt-96-a-leader-in-international-adoptions. html

Dubois, L. (2012). *Haiti: The aftershocks of history.* New York: Metropolitan Books.

Duster, T. (2001). Buried alive: The concept of race in science. *The Chronicle of Higher Education* 48(3): B11–12.

Eske, A. (2010). *My family, a symphony: A memoir of global adoption.* New York: Palgrave.

Gravatar21. (2011, August 11). A critique of Harry and Bertha Holt's work while setting up intercountry adoption in South Korea. [Web log post]. Retrieved from http://

transracialeyes.com/2011/08/11/a-brief-historical-overview-of-the-life-and-times-of-har-ry-and-bertha-holt-and-the-origin-of-international-adoption/ Accessed August 19, 2019.

Holt, M. (1992). *The orphan trains: Placing out in America*. Lincoln & London: University of Nebraska Press.

Hubinette, T. (2006). From orphan trains to babylifts: Colonial trafficking, empire building, and social engineering. In: Outsiders within: Writing on transracial adoption, Boston: South End Press , p. 139-149

Hubinette, T. & Arvanitakis, J. (2012). Transracial adoption, White cosmopolitanism and the fantasy of the global family. *Third Text* 26(6): 691–703.

Katz, J. (2013). *The big truck that went by*. New York: Palgrave Macmillan.

Kennedy, R. (2003). *Interracial intimacies: Sex, marriage, identity, and adoption*. New York: Vintage Books. pp 389–392.

Kirton, D. (2000). *'Race', ethnicity and adoption*. Buckingham, England: Open University Press.

Mesirow, J, (2009). Transformative learning theory. In J. Mesirow, and E. W. Taylor (Eds.), *Transformative learning in practice: Insights from community, workplace, and higher education*. Hoboken, NJ: Wiley & Sons, Inc.

National Association of Black Social Workers. (1972). *Position paper on trans-racial adoptions*. New York: NABSW.

National Association of Black Social Workers. (1991). *Preserving African American families*. New York: NABSW. pp.4

National Association of Black Social Workers (2003). *Preserving families of African ancestry*. New York: NABSW.

Patton, S. (2000). *Birthmarks: Transracial adoption in contemporary America*. New York: New York University Press.

Reitz, W. (2010). Reflections on the special humanitarian parole program for Haitian orphans. *New York Law School Review* 55:791–798.

Simon R., Altstein, H. & Melli, M. (1994). *The case for transracial adoption*. Washington, DC: The American University Press.

Smith, D. (April, 12, 2012) Transracial adoption blog. http://www.darronsmith.com/2012/04/is-love-enough-exploring-white-understandings-about-race-and-the-limits-of-whiteness-in-transracial-adoptions-by-dr-darron-t-smith/

Smith, D., Cardell, J. & Juarez, B. (2011). *White parents, Black children: Exploring transracial adoption*. New York: Rowan & Littlefield Publishers.

U.S. Citizenship and Immigration Services (2010). Special humanitarian parole program for Haitian orphan fact sheet. Retrieved from PDF www.aila.org File download embedded file

University of Oregon, Department of History. (2012, February 12). The adoption history project: Bertha and Harry Holt. http://darkwing.uoregon.edu/~adoption/people/holt.htm

Wexler, L. (2000). *Tender violence: Domestic visions in an age of U.S. imperialism*. Chapel Hill: University of North Carolina Press.

· 2 ·

FLATLANDS, BROOKLYN

"To be one of Brooklyn's estimated 2.6 million residents is to be a person who constantly encounters and is accepting of people different from oneself."

William B. Helmreich

Brooklyn is the most populous of the five boroughs of New York City with its over 2 million people living on 71 square miles of the most southwestern portion of Long Island. The population density is 37,137 people per square mile. Residents come from all seven continents of the world with 37 % foreign born and 22 % of residents living below the poverty line (US Census, 2010).

The native people of Brooklyn were the Canarsie tribe of Lenape who were part of the Delaware Nation. They were hunters and gatherers specializing in fishing and fur trade. Some assimilated into the European communities that immigrated, or moved from Brooklyn to Staten Island, New Jersey or Pennsylvania. Sadly, those of the Canarsie tribe who remained were killed by the Dutch settlers (Manbeck, 2019).

In the 1600s the original European settlers were Dutch, and they gave Brooklyn its name, Brueklen (brew-clenn) named after a village in the Netherlands. After the Dutch, the English came and anglicized the name to Brooklyn we know it today (Goode, 2018).

In the 1700s, Brooklyn's inhabitants included Dutch, German, English, French and Scandinavians, and slaves brought from Africa. Slavery abounded in these villages called Kings County, and in the late 1770s slaves made up almost one half of the population who worked the farmlands. During this time New York City, or Manhattan Island as it was called then, was flourishing as was Brooklyn because it was the way food from the rich soils of Long Island passed to the City (Thirteen, n.d.).

Brooklyn became an official borough of the City of New York in 1898. From its beginnings, Brooklyn has had its share of urban strife, a wide range of cultures and socioeconomic statuses. It has always been relatively over-crowded and much of its population, poor. By 1900, Brooklyn's population increased by over a million people, and it was the third largest and fastest growing city in the US (Keilholtz, 2016).

A large group of European immigrants often called the "first wave" came to Brooklyn in the mid-1800s when Irish peasants escaping fam-ine, and Germans escaping a failed revolution, came. The so-called sec-ond wave took place in the late 1800s consisting of Italians, Russian Jews, Poles, Swedes, Norwegians, Danes and Finns. The next wave occurred between World War 1 and the 1930s and was known as the Great Migration when Blacks from the south moved north to Harlem then on to Brooklyn (Thirteen, n.d.).

In the early 1900s, Brooklyn was a hub for industry and manufacturing with the Brooklyn Navy Yard bustling. But by the 1950s heavy manufacturers and industries started to move to less expensive places where the harbors were deeper. White middle-class residents abandoned Brooklyn for Queens, Long Island and Staten Island. New immigrants continued to come to Brooklyn, however, from the Caribbean, Puerto Rico, Latin America, China, Korea, the Soviet Union, and the Middle East. The 1970s and 1980s were turbulent times in Brooklyn—high crime, decay, poverty, drugs, gangs, and despair. But in the 1990s the tide began to turn and neighborhoods in Brooklyn began to spring back (Thirteen, n.d.). It seems Brooklyn has always been an immigrant land from which first generation migrants come and settle, then their chil-dren or grandchildren spread out to other states in America. These immigrant populations have left their imprint on Brooklyn, thus being born in Brooklyn or living in its neighborhoods for any length of time in turn leaves its imprint on you.

Joni

Brooklyn is home to me. Yes, New York in general but Brooklyn in particular. It is amazing how many roads run through Brooklyn, how many people have relationships, connections and history in this place. I love the languages, the cultures and the foods. But I especially love the kindness, the intensity and did I say, kindness—yes, the kindness. Kindness is not a word frequently associated with New York City but that has been my experience. Yes, I was mugged once but despite that one occurrence I have always felt safe in Brooklyn as safe as anywhere else in America.

Rebecca

Do I consider Brooklyn home? That's a really good question. No. I would consider New York home because that is where family is, where my friends are, and where I will probably return. I don't consider Gulu my home, right now, either. Now I have a place in Gulu where I live but not a home. I think it is the people that make the home, the relationships. I think my home will be where my children and husband are when I am married. That will be home then.

I do see how Brooklyn has influenced me, shaped me. It is the music I play in the dance class I teach. Yes, I am definitely a city girl. Brooklyn is still in me.

Joni

Brooklyn is in me as well. It is funny how a place can be in you, how you not only inhabit a place, but the place inhabits you. Brooklyn is that kind of space. What were your first impressions?

Rebecca

I don't know. I was nine years old. New smells, new people, different, urban. It was cold. I was never around the cold before. My clothes were inappropriate for the cold weather, and I was unprepared. At the first snow fall, I was excited but then the colder it got the drier my skin became. That's what I recall. And then I really didn't have time to adjust, none of us did Nathan and Matthew, my new adopted brothers, either. This was the situation we were thrown into. We all just had to accept. These were my siblings; this was my family; this was my home—I just had to adjust. But I didn't self-identify with Brooklyn and just love it like Nate did; not like Nate who self-identified with Brooklyn.

Self- identify. How do I self-identify? I'm African American. I am an African American woman; that is how I self-identify. My priority when I first came to learn English. I just learned it but not by going to a school or taking tutoring. If I am immersed in a culture, I just learn it. I speak French. I learn the patterns, the way it works, and you do this first then the rest follows. I just spoke English. It just clicks in my brain; French, Spanish, Creole, and Dutch. When I was younger, we learned Spanish, French, and English at the orphanage. Coming to the US, English was my priority. I said to myself that I have to learn English. No one corrected my English. Then in 8th grade at New Hope Academy, I was learning Spanish; and the teacher asked, "Are you Dominican? You have the accent and everything." I said "no." I have a really good ear for languages, and especially if I just live in a place, I will pick up the language. I remember when I was in Holland, and I picked up Dutch. My host mother said teasingly, "Now, we can't talk behind your back anymore!"

Looking back on my middle years in Brooklyn, I don't think I would raise children there—well, maybe but in a different way. I am not saying that you did anything wrong. I would just not raise them in an all-Black neighborhood. I want them to be in an affluent neighborhood. I know that sounds bad, but I want my children in well-equipped schools, to be around well-educated children from well-educated families. It sounds really stuck up and snobby, but I like museums and art galleries. I do remember girls saying, "You are so stuck up, and she dresses like a White girl! She's such a White girl in a Black girl's body." So, I didn't have friends. From that experience, I learned that I want my kids to be exposed to the world and have a global perspective. I want my kids to be exposed to cultural activities and other races and people. Our schools, Bay Ridge Christian Academy and New Hope, were ok. But they didn't really provide that exposure and challenge. People did just ok.

Joni

We chose Bay Ridge Christian Academy and New Hope Christian Academy, in the late 1980s and early 1990s because we wanted you to be safe, and we were not sure if you would be in the public schools. We also wanted you to have a Christian foundation. I think your Dad and I may have been misguided and short-sighted; we probably could have found really excellent public schools that provided more challenge and intellectual opportunity and safety, but we did the best we could with where we were with our thinking and spiritual growth at the time.

Moving from a small town in Minnesota to New York in 1978, New York was a scary place—high crime, a lot of drugs, frequent acts of violence—heroin, crack, cocaine. We found an apartment at the bottom of Park Slope between 4th

and 5th Avenues on Degraw Street before any of that part of Brooklyn was gentrified. Degraw had been an Italian neighborhood and then became mostly Puerto
Rican, Dominican and Central American. We rented a third-floor apartment of a
brownstone for only $90 a month in 1978 because nobody wanted to live in that
neighborhood. The rent was really low even for those days. The story has it that
our Italian landlords who had grown up on the block when it was mostly Italian,
and whose mother still lived a few doors down on Degraw, really wanted a "nice
young White couple." That was us. Newly married, we had come to New York
because we believed, and still do, that we had been directed by God. On that block
our car was broken into on a regular basis with the radio ripped out and stolen, the
spare tire and whatever else could be removed was taken. We were also mugged
once in Bushwick when I was pregnant with Nathan; we weren't seriously hurt
but the fear stuck for a while. These experiences affected the choice of schools we
placed you in.

We moved to Sunset Park after Matthew was born and stayed in a rented place
when there were still some Scandinavians living there before the 1980s when the

Figure 2.1   Matthew, Rebecca, Nathan—siblings

Chinese moved in, and Sunset Park became Brooklyn's first Chinatown. The apartment house that was our home is now a Chinese day care. Then there was Flatlands which was your first home in the US. We moved to Flatlands in 1989 and you were adopted in 1990.

Flatlands

The neighborhood of Flatlands is in the southeast part of the borough of Brooklyn with the boundaries of Avenue H on the north, Ralph Avenue on the east, Avenues T and Flatlands Avenue south, and Flatbush Avenue and Nostrand Avenue on the west. Today it is a mostly Black population, predominantly Caribbean with a strong Haitian contingent. It was annexed to the borough of Brooklyn in 1896. As previously stated, it originally was inhabited by the Lenape meaning *the People*; this included the Canarsie and Nayacks. Then in the 1600s the Dutch came and founded the five villages of: Bushwick, Brooklyn, Flatbush, Flatlands, and New Utrecht.

Flatlands has most often been a bedroom community, designed for raising a family, with most inhabitants working in Manhattan and commuting to this two-fare zone. At one time it was a White population, consisting mostly of Italians, Jews, the Irish who left in the 1970s and 1980s in White flight (the phenomenon of White people moving out of urban areas when minority populations move in) for the suburbs. So, when many Black families moved in, predominantly from Caribbean countries into this middle-class neighborhood there was a mixture of suspicion, fear, and slow acceptance by the remaining Whites (Helmreich, 2016).

Today Flatlands is approximately 66.3% Black, mostly of Caribbean descent, 18.2% White and 9% Latino and a smattering of other groups. (US Census 2010). Between 2000 and 2015, Flatlands was one of only a few neighborhoods in Brooklyn with an increase in African American populations with 38,711 Blacks moving in and 19,832 Whites moving out (Small, 2017) of Flatlands and adjoining Canarsie. According to one Flatlands resident, Flatlands "hasn't been discovered yet" (Hymowech, 2016)—that means that gentrification has not "hit" it like other parts of Brooklyn. This might be because it is a two-fare zone. Travel to the City usually means you need to take a bus and a subway ride. Or maybe gentrification is kept at bay because there are many Black middle- class homeowners who are holding on to their properties. According to one popular urban travel expert and writer, "It's neighborhoods like these that challenge the stereotype of Black communities as poor, crime ridden, and rundown. Many of the residents are sitting on their porches, relaxing, chatting with friends and relatives, minding their own business, and perhaps yours if you stick around a bit too long" (Helmreich, 2016, p. 251).

Joni

When I think of Flatlands and East 48th Street, I have very fond memories, especially of my still best friend, Valerie, who lived next door, and my West Indian, Latino, and longtime Jewish neighbors. I remember curried goat, block parties with open fire hydrants of spurting water on hot days, street basketball, and sitting on the front stoop talking to neighbors and knowing almost everyone on the block. It was and is a community, a family.

Two stories stick out in my mind, the first is a cab ride conversation and the second is the ice cream truck. One evening soon after moving to Flatlands, I rode a cab home and the White driver, and I started up a conversation. After asking me my address, he asked how long I had lived there. I said we had just moved in a few weeks prior. I will never forget what he said, "Are you kidding me? Why did you buy in this neighborhood? All the other Whites are moving out. Why would you live here?" I don't remember what I said, but I do remember feeling sad. I had heard of White flight when people of color moved into neighborhoods, but I had never heard it put so bluntly nor did your Dad and I ever consider who lived in the neighborhood—it just wasn't part of our way of seeing the world.

Rebecca

What I remember of 1315 East 48th Street was that I had friends, but they were not my real friends. The girls were so catty. There was some fight going on every year; Black girls fighting Black girls; Black boys, too. My experience was that always there was something with Black children. Often on the block it seemed there was someone saying, "There is going to be a fight." I was not into it. I didn't have that mindset; Blacks fighting Blacks and enjoying it.

I have Black girlfriends now. They are mostly professional women, and we are supportive and encouraging of each other. But my experience, perhaps beginning in Flatlands, is that with some Black women there is jealousy and competition, putting you down. There was, for me, girls saying, "You think you're better than us"; this kind of bullying that I couldn't stand. Bullying every year especially when we came home from holiday, and we came back to the block. There would be gossip while I was gone.

Shaqueeda would bad mouth and say to the girls on the block that I said really bad things about them that I never said. Especially one year in the 8th grade when we spent five weeks in Maine, when I came back to the block, I said "Hi everybody" but the girls wouldn't talk to me. Shaqueeda made up lies about me. So, when I came home none of the girls on the block talked to me. One girl, Marlene, told me what Shaqueeda did. Marlene said that Shaqueeda told the girls I gossiped awful stories about each girl which I didn't. Marlene was the only one who remained my friend. This happened every summer.

So, when I went to Fontbonne Hall Academy, the all-White Catholic girls prep high school, I thought, I don't need the girls on the block as my friends. I thought I have a life outside this block. One summer I went to a pool with my White friends from Fontbonne in Breezy Point, a gated White community in another part of Brooklyn. Year after year the bullying and aggressive behavior continued, and I felt picked on for no reason. Even to this day, the memories linger with me. I hear words like, "She thinks she is better than us. She has White friends. Finally, I determined "I'm finished. I need to shut her mouth for good this time. And I did it."

I think the whole thing came to a head when I went to a pool party with my friends from Fontbonne, and I wanted to dry my hair. I went to retrieve my dryer from Shaqueeda who had borrowed it. Well, she broke it. I was so upset. I had had enough. I called her that "fucking fat bitch, and this bitch needs to stop fuckin' with me. I will shove that dryer up her ass." I let her know I'm done; I'm finished in front of everyone on the block because they were so nosey and were watching. You told me to get inside the house and stop screaming. I was shouting on the street, and then I called the police on her.

Joni

Yes, I remember well. All of a sudden, after you went into your bedroom a police car drove up to the front of our house and walked to our front door. I said, "Why are you here?" They said that someone from this house called the police. I said, "Ohhh, come with me. I think I know who called. The two male officers came to your bedroom, and you proceeded to tell them about Shaqueeda breaking the hair dryer. Thank God the officers were pretty level-headed and just tried to calm you down. When you did not seem to be getting through to them about the severity of the hair dryer incident, you said, "And my mom grabbed my arm." I had in fact grabbed your arm when trying to get you to calm down and go to your room.

Rebecca

I didn't say that you were hitting me, just that you grabbed my arm. But I guess I finally shut her ass up. I thought I am done with this bullying. That is really where all the anger came from not the broken hair dryer. I had had enough. I didn't tell you and Dad about the bullying because I didn't feel you defended me. You always seemed to agree with everyone else and say, "Yes, Rebecca is like that." You sided on the side of the other person whenever anyone said anything negative about me. I didn't feel I could go to you for defense. She brought other girls from another block to fight. You didn't believe anything I said anyway. So annoying was the bullying on East 48th Street. She pissed me off.

Joni

I am sorry that you felt you couldn't tell me and that I didn't listen. I am sorry that I did not know enough, did not do enough homework about older adoptive children. I am sorry I did not support you the way a mother should have. Yes, in some ways I did the best I could, but I think knowing what I know now, I could have been more empathetic, more supportive, more help to you. For that I am sorry.

Rebecca

That whole thing—my experience and the bullying is a big thing. See how angry I still am after 25 years? Then I remember when you cut my hair really short, so I looked like a boy. I will never cut my hair like that again. You said that it was going to look so nice, but it didn't. I looked like a boy because it was so short, and I was always a "girlie girl." When you cut it, I felt forced to do that, and I felt like a boy with that haircut. I hated it. I was mistaken for a boy several times, and I was once bullied about that too. Yes, I looked horrible and that made me very angry.

Joni

Yes, I had trouble doing your hair properly, and that is why we cut it so short so as to manage it. I probably did that after the day I dropped you off at Bay Ridge Christian Academy, and a Black mother walked over to my car and handed me a plastic bag full of Black hair products including shea butter moisturizing hair treatment, cocoa and castor shampoos and conditioners. When I opened the bag and saw the hair products, I cried and was so mad. How dare that woman imply that I can't take care of my own daughter's hair? Even though, I couldn't. I thought at the time, if I were not a White mother, she never would have had the gall to insinuate that I couldn't take care of my daughter's hair. This incident just reinforced my insecurities as a mother, in particular as the mother of a Black child. It was probably then that I decided to have your hair cut short. Later as the years went by, I understood that the woman just meant well. She wanted to help me, and she thought she was doing me a favor. If I knew then what I know now, I would have thanked her and asked her for help and advice. But I was too insecure about my mothering at the time.

Rebecca

Well, I was just happy to grow up and do my hair myself. I never wore it short again. In fact, I usually kept it really long and still do. I am still that girlie girl. I love to be feminine; I love pretty clothes, sexy shoes, and lacey lingerie. That is still me.

Joni

You taught me to be feminine and helped me discover the feminine side of me. If you remember, you would examine what I put on some days, and say "Oh, Mom, that does not look good—wear this." We were the same size and still are. We wore each other's clothes, but mostly I wore your clothes because you had better taste then me. I learned from you. Now people say I am a classy dresser, and I know how to accessorize. Well, that came from you.

Going back to how I didn't defend you, I do remember though, one time I did defend you, and I got it right. It was a late sunny afternoon in summer on East 48th Street, and I was sitting on our stoop porch reading. You were playing with friends, in particular that day a boy named James who was about eleven years old like you. An ice cream truck slowly approached the block with its monotonous tinkling music that you could hear from blocks away so that children had plenty of time to ask parents for money or collect their nickels and dimes. You heard it and immediately ran up the stoop steps and asked for money for ice cream. I flatly said "no" as dinnertime was soon, and I didn't want you to spoil your appetite. You were visibly annoyed. Little did I know at that moment, James was watching the whole transaction between us. Disappointed you returned to the street and James, where I watched what seemed to be a heated discussion between the two of you. After a few minutes, you ran back up the stoop this time telling me that James said that the reason that I would not buy you ice cream was because I was not your real mother.

I had an immediate visceral reaction. I stood up and summoned James up to the stoop where he stood in front of me as I proceeded to lecture him. It went something like this: "James, look at me—see this arm, (pinching the skin of my arm together)

I am real. I am the woman who tucks Rebecca into bed and kisses her goodnight. I am the woman who helps her with her homework, who makes sure she eats her meals, dresses her and helps her with her bath. I take care of her when she is sick; I discipline her when she is bad; I worry about her when she is sad. That is real, and I am her real mother. I am not the woman who gave her birth but nevertheless I am her real mom. So, don't you ever say that again!"

As I finished, James was nodding yes with a fearful look on his face, and you were standing behind me with a huge grin on your face as if to say, "I guess she told him!"

A mother's job is to defend her child. I guess sometimes I succeeded and sometimes I failed.

Orphan Trains

Growing up in Brooklyn, there was frequently the possibility of witnessing a mugging on the subway, hearing roosters crow in the morning or an occasional gunshot at night, or seeing people become loud, drunk or violent. It included frequently experiencing the homeless on the subways or street asking for help. These are things that happen in crowded urban spaces. Life as a child growing up on the streets of Brooklyn can be rough; to be born and raised in Brooklyn requires resilience. This was certainly true for the children of the Orphan Train (Blakemore, 2019).

Between 1854 and 1929, approximately 200,000 children from New York, many of them from Brooklyn who were abandoned, orphaned, or given up by families who could not afford to raise them, were part of a great experiment. Brooklyn at this time was overcrowded and poor, and many families could not afford to support their children. The Orphan Train was an actual train and project to relocate urban children, mostly White children, to Midwest families to be adopted, put in foster care, or taken in to work on the farms of Iowa, Missouri, Kansas, Illinois and other farm regions. At this time, some states did not have adoption policies and procedures and others did not have child-protection laws. So, for some children of the Orphan Train this arrangement worked well; for others not so well (Warren, 1998).

Among the hundreds of unique stories is that of Clinton Simpson, a boy from Brooklyn and part of the Orphan Train that left Grand Central Station on November 10, 1913 for Waukon a small town in the Allamakee County of Iowa. He was not a *real* orphan. His father was killed in a carriage accident on the streets of New York, and his mother could not feed him and his younger sister. So, she gave him up when he was fourteen years old, hoping that he would be adopted by a family in the Midwest and have a better chance at a decent life away from Brooklyn. From Simpson's notes, his descendants pieced together what this was like for an adolescent at the time:

> Grand Central Station was majestic and seductive, but Clinton was never more transfixed than when his cheek pressed into his mother's bosom in the midst of her endless hug on the morning of November 10, 1913. She showed up to see him off and say one final good-bye. Her tears dripped onto the brim of his secondhand bowler . . . He climbed aboard the steam engine and dared not look back. It was the only way he could avoid crying (Keilholtz, 2016, p. 39).

It was the last time he saw his mother. Later as a young adult, he tried to contact her and pay for his sister and mother to come from Brooklyn to Iowa, but his mother died before she was scheduled to visit Iowa, and Clinton didn't even have the finances to go and bury her. His sister then disappeared, and he never saw her again. Initially, when in Iowa on the Orphan Train, a rich widower took him in as an extra farm hand. The widower gave him no fatherly nurturance. He was later relocated and adopted, although not officially, into a more loving farm family who needed an extra farm hand but who also loved him. Although Clinton missed his mother and sister and Brooklyn, the Orphan Train experiment was a relatively good one for him, but this would not be the case for all children (Keilholtz, 2016).

On the train ride from Brooklyn to Iowa the children were sandwiched in like sardines and motion sickness was common. There were babies and children of all ages up to adolescents like Clinton Simpson. Once arriving in Iowa where the town had prepared for the event and were expected, the children were placed on something like an auction block with many hundreds of potential adoptive, foster parents, and spectators gawking and bidding for the children. Some adoptive parents had already made applications for children, but others had not. All came up to the auction stage for the selection process which included an inspection of the children. The adults opened the orphans' mouths to look at their teeth, hiked the little girls' skirts up to inspect their legs, and used a measuring tape to check their height. The children were treated like pieces of meat (Keilholtz, 2016).

The babies were taken first leaving the older children to be chosen later. The older children did have a say. If they didn't want to go with a family, they could say no. But often they were too scared, or concerned that they would never have a family at all to say no. Right before the auction display, the children were fed, washed and given fresh clothes to wear before being paraded like cattle through the selection process.

Rebecca

There were no auction blocks for us; I guess it was much more humane. The potential adoptive parents came to Christian Haitian Outreach Orphanage (CHO) in Carrefour to see the children. Eleanor Workman, an African American woman, started CHO in 1974 when she found a terminally ill mother with her twin babies living on a garbage dump because she could not pay her rent. Before the mother died, she gave guardianship of the twins to Mom Workman, and I was told that is how CHO started.

There were several hundred of us, I think. The potential parents played with all the kids. It wasn't out in the open. The parents then talked to Mom Workman and said, "This is the child that I want." Mom Workman spoke little Creole but was a very good woman with a deep faith in God and commitment to the children. We were all afraid of her but in a reverent sort of way. It was all pretty secretive, so I don't know who the children were or who the adoptive parents were. I suspect the babies were adopted quicker. I don't remember a lot of kids being adopted. I just don't remember. Some of the kids I grew up with are now adults in Haiti, especially the older boys. The wave of adoption came after I left in 1990. That's when everyone else started leaving. A lot went to Canada because some parents adopted children who had siblings and only a few to the US. My recollection of the day I found out I was leaving was when Mom Workman was not around. I think Elsie Lherisson or Sister Karen told me. Elsie was a Haitian-born American who had worked on Wall Street but decided to return to Haiti to work with the children doing missionary work. Sister Karen was a White missionary from the Southern U.S. Mom Workman didn't tell me. I remember you came twice, and Dad came once.

Joni

I have a different recollection and understanding. My recollection of being at the orphanage after we had "chosen" you is that we were sitting in Mom Workman's office and she brought you in. You were a skinny and beautiful nine-year old. You stood in front of all three of us, me, your dad, and Mom Workman. Mom said to you, "Mr. and Mrs. Schwartz want to be your mommy and daddy." I remember you said nothing, and you didn't even have a non-verbal response. Perhaps that is because you already knew and were not surprised. At that moment, I wondered if you wanted us. Mom Workman then told you to give us each a kiss and you did. Then you walked out of the room. I remember feeling apprehensive and a little anxious that perhaps you were unhappy with this turn of events.

But a few minutes later, we walked out to the open courtyard where all the children ran and played, and it was clear that all the children knew that we were adopting you. You had spread the word! They all ran to us with outstretched arms, jumping on us, and shouting "Adopt me, too! Adopt me, too!"

Rebecca

Then I remember the plane trip to New York's JFK airport. Taking off the ground, my stomach was going down to the ground, and I was screaming and squealing and everyone on the plane was laughing; the stewardess and the passengers. I don't remember arriving at the airport. I guess I do remember wearing the yellow dress. Then there was my new home, 1315 East 48th Street, Flatlands, Brooklyn, my Dad, my brothers—Nathan and Matthew. It was October 11, 1990, my Dad's birthday and my adoption birthday. I never looked back much until now.

References

Blakemore, E. (2019, January 28). 'Orphan trains' brought homeless NYC children to work on farms out west. History website. Retrieved May 14, 2019—https://www.history.com/news/orphan-trains-childrens-aid-society

Goode, K. (2018) How Brooklyn got its name TripSavvy online blog. www.tripsavvy.com/how-did-brooklyn-get-its-name-443093. Access March 9, 2019.

Helmreich, W. (2016). The Brooklyn nobody knows: An urban walking guide. Princeton, NJ: Princeton University Press.

Hymowech, G. (2016, June 22) Flatlands, the forgotten Brooklyn neighborhood. https://beforeitsgone.co/stories/1XIBqT. Access March 10, 2019.

Keilholtz, J. (2016). A boy from Brooklyn: Clinton Simpson and the orphan train. North Charleston, SC: CreateSpace.

Manbeck, J. (May 9, 2019). Ask a historian: What happened to Brooklyn's Native American tribes? The Brooklyn Eagle. www.brooklneagle.com/articles/2019/05/02/ask-a-historian-what-happened-to-brooklyn-native-american-tribes/

Small, A. (2017, May 5). Mapping the modern transformation of New York City. CityLab https://www.citylab.com/life/2017/mapping-the-transforamtion-of-new-york-city/525330/

Thirteen (n.d) History of Brooklyn. https://www.thirteen.org/brooklyn/history/history3.html

US Census (2010). https://www.census.gov/quickfacts/kingscountybrooklynboroughnewyork

Warren, A. (1998). The orphan train. The Washington Post. Retrieved May 14, 2019 https://www.washingtonpost.com/wp-srv/national/horizon/nov98/orphan.htm

· 3 ·

MINNETONKA, MINNESOTA

"Either America will destroy ignorance or ignorance will destroy the US."
W.E.B. DuBois

Growing up in the 1950s and 60s in Minnetonka, Joni learned to swim in Lake Minnetonka and spent nearly every day on its banks. She spent the first third of her life in Minnetonka, moving to New York with her then husband, Paul, when she was 26 years old. Rebecca visited her grandmother in Minnetonka and spent some months of 2011 at the Humphrey School of Public Affairs at the University of Minnesota studying for a master's degree.

Ironically, Rebecca later worked overseas, and the organization she worked for *The Center for Victims of Torture* is headquartered in Minnesota. Then and now, Minnetonka, on the banks of a large lake is an affluent almost exclusively White suburb of Minneapolis which has informed our life experiences. "You experience places and learn, if attentive about processes and relationships in those places" (Deloria &Wildcat, 2001. pg. 36). The Minnesota Dakota proverb "*We will forever be known by the tracks we leave*" seems to speak to the power of place to tell stories. These stories have left a few tracks in us as well.

Native American Tracks

The names *Minnetonka* and *Minnesota* came from the Dakota Indians. But the very first Minnesota settlers, 7000–9000 years ago, were the Paleo-Indians, then the Dakota and the Ojibwa- Chippewa arrived from the north and east to inhabit the now Midwestern state of Minnesota (Unze, 2011). For hundreds of years the Ojibwe and Dakota co-inhabited this territory while engaging in ongoing warfare (Reicher, 2018).

The name Minnesota came from the Dakota word, mnisota, literally meaning cloudy water referencing the Minnesota River. Minnetonka came from mini tanka meaning *great water* after the large and beautiful Lake Minnetonka. Minneapolis, one of the twin cities of Minnesota, came from Mne ha-ha (waterfall) and the Greek word for city "polis" thus the City of Waters (Upham, 2001). While wars and conflict such as the Dakota Uprising of 1862 and the Battle of Shakopee in 1858 (Unze, 2011; Reicher, 2018) as well as intra-tribal warfare were part of life at that time, Lake Minnetonka was spared. This lake was considered sacred and holy ground by the Dakota (Excelsior-Lake Minnetonka Historical Society; Allyn, 2015) and thereby because of its spiritual significance was kept hallowed by the indigenous tribes in spite of the battles (Allyn, 2015).

W.E.B. DuBois and Lake Minnetonka

Lake Minnetonka is notable for another little-known historical fact. W.E.B. Dubois, the African American philosopher, scholar and great civil rights leader of the 20th Century, spent the summer of 1888 between his graduation from Fisk University and attending graduate school at Harvard, on Lake Minnetonka at the monstrous Hotel Lafayette built in 1882 by James J. Hill, the railroad mogul (Meyer, 2003). In the 1880s Lake Minnetonka hotels, like the Lafayette, were huge luxury structures for European royalist, former American presidents, and elite, affluent Whites from across the country and the world. The Hotel Lafayette, the "Saratoga of the West" was a decadent location for only the wealthiest and was five stories high with verandas that encircled the hotel. New railroad systems and steamboats made access to the hotel possible. It was one of several grand hotels for Whites only of the era. It burned to the ground in 1897 (Dregni, 2014).

Dubois worked that summer in the Hotel Lafayette's kitchen. Dubois raised money for his tuition to Harvard by singing on Friday evenings at the Lafayette with the Fisk Glee Club (The Minneapolis Tribune, 1888). It is thought that it was this summer that helped him conceptualize his theory of *double consciousness*. As defined by DuBois in his classic 1903 book, *The Souls of Black Folk*, double consciousness is "this sense of always looking at one's self through the eyes of others ... one ever feels his two-ness, an American, a Negro; two souls, two thoughts, two unreconciled strivings; two warring ideals in one dark body, whose dogged strength alone keeps it from being torn asunder" (p. 2–3). This theory encompasses the internal contradictions and psychological challenges experienced by marginalized groups within racist societies (DuBois, 1903). DuBois briefly describes this summer in his book, *Dusk of Dawn: An Essay toward an Autobiography of a Race Concept* (2007):

> After graduation, the members of the Fisk Glee Club went to Lake Minnetonka, a resort in Minnesota, for the summer of 1888, with the idea of working in the dining room and giving concerts . . .. The only difficulty about the Minnesota excursion was that I had never worked in a hotel in my life; I could not wait on tables and therefore became one of the bus boys. It was so unusual a pageant to watch the dining room that I made no tips and for a long time had difficulty in getting enough to eat, not realizing that in that day servants in great hotels were not systematically fed but foraged for food in devious ways. I saw Americans, rich and near-rich, at play; it was not inspiring. The servility necessary for the successful waiter I could not or would not learn (p. 17).

Ogland (2001), in his book, *Picturing Lake Minnetonka*, also refers to DuBois's "tensions" on his job at the Lafayette. According to Ogland, most waiters were either African American or immigrant Italians and all guests were White elite or near elites. The waiters and busboys were fed only the scraps from meals. Serving these large meals and seeing the wastefulness, while the staff went hungry, was extremely hard for DuBois to bear. In his words, there was an "assumption that worker and diner had no common humanity." One particular guest, summoned for DuBois's services and the way in which this guest beckoned him would never be forgotten:

> It was not his voice, for his mouth was too full. It was his way, his air, his assumption. Thus, Caesar ordered his legionaries or Cleopatra her slaves. Dogs recognized the gesture. I did not. He may be beckoning yet for all I know, for something froze within me. I did not look his way again. Then and there I disowned menial service for me and my people (DuBois, 1920, p. 112).

According to Minnesotan playwright, Kim Hines, who wrote a 2001 play based on Dubois's summer at the Lafayette entitled *Summer in the Shadows*, and whose father knew the adult Dubois while doing graduate work in Atlanta:

> All of DuBois' Black Nationalism and Pan-African thoughts and philosophies came much later in his life. *Summer in the Shadows* takes place during a time before he really knew himself as a Black man in America. Having lived his childhood in a town of less than 5,000 people [in New England] (of whom only 50 residents were Black)-- and not knowing what it was like to be around a large number of Black people until he went away to college at Fisk University in Nashville--he really had no sense of himself in a much larger context (Play Summer in the Shadows, 2001).

Then there was Lake Minnetonka, Minnesota, the Hotel Lafayette and the summer of 1888. This time was a disorienting dilemma for DuBois and began to shape his thinking and outlook on race, racism, White supremacy, and double consciousness going forward. *Summer in the Shadows* is a fictionalized version of what happened that summer based upon a DuBois's short story, *Vacation Unique* (Zamir, 1995). From the story and Hines's father's association with DuBois, DuBois's other writings, and research on his life' Hines pieced together a very probable drama of that summer (Hines, K., personal communication, October 29, 2018). One of the more poignant portions of the play comes near the end when Dubois (Willie) will be leaving soon, and he decides to swim in the lake, a strictly forbidden act for "coloreds":

> WILLIE (DuBois): . . . I started thinking how refreshing it would be to dip my body into Minnetonka Lake (almost whispers almost in a trance) Minnetonka Lake . . . White folks Lake . . . Minnetonka . . . Minnetonka . . . Minnetonka. The more I thought about it, the more the heat started to come up off my skin. And then I thought about the cool wetness of the water . . . and how nice it would be to cool myself down . . . and why I couldn't just immerse myself . . . (pause) And before I really knew what was happening, my clothes were fully off and I was floating. Floating in the middle of the lake (slight pause). This is what it must feel like to be White (p.87).

Joni

I love to swim. I have extremely strong memories and impressions of swimming in Lake Minnetonka. I never noticed it was in a wealthy community or all White. I was a child and the waters embraced me and made me feel light and dreamy and free. Again, as I write I am smacked once more about what I do not know whether from erasure, poor schooling or my own intellectual laziness. Growing up in Minnetonka, swimming in the lake every summer and skating and ice fishing on it when it was frozen over, I did not know its history. Who swam in those waters before me? Those sacred waters.

As a child I could not get enough of the water. I watched the thermometer on awaking every morning to see it rise to 65 degrees because at 65 degrees swimming lessons would be on, the beach opened, and my mother let me take my bicycle the 1.2 miles which took about 7 minutes to the water. My summer vacation rallied between the library and checking out stacks of books every two weeks, reading all of them; and swimming.

I learned to swim in Lake Minnetonka. I still remember the first time I was able to float on my stomach and on my back; I felt light as air, I trusted the world, the water, my body; floating gave me faith that there was a larger force upholding me. And yes, as DuBois must have felt—it gave me freedom. And, it is no surprise to me that DuBois conceptualized his double-consciousness theory in Minnetonka.

Rebecca

Minnetonka, I wasn't there much. I went to visit Minnetonka when we visited grandma or when Aunt Elsie took us there. That was when I was a child, and my family was White, so I was with them and felt accepted.

As a young adult, I returned for graduate school and lived in Minnesota for one year. I hated it there. I felt isolated, lonely, and I didn't feel that I fit in. At first, I thought it was me, but since then I have met Whites, even some from Minnesota, who say they had trouble making friends there as well. People seem to have their own friends. Many grew up there, didn't leave, and it was hard to make friends with them. Whereas other places I have lived, there are expats and many people who didn't grow up in the location, so we identified and became friends.

During my enrollment in the Humphrey Graduate Program of the University of Minnesota, I remember one incident that really stuck out for me. I remember I met this girl, a Black girl from Minnesota, and I could tell she didn't like me. Eventually we became friends and she said, "I didn't like you when I first met you." I said, "I know. Why?" "Because I saw you talking to a group of White people and you looked so comfortable when you were with them, and they looked so comfortable with you. But then when I saw you talking to LaToya, I knew you were ok. If LaToya is friends with you, then you are ok." "You had a Black woman vet me to tell you I am ok?" I questioned. Then I further responded, "If a White person says racists stuff, I am the first person to point it out, and you wouldn't do it. I am the first one to stand up, and I confront it. You have seen me do it, and you wouldn't." She countered,

"That's because you are from New York." I said, "Coming from New York has nothing to do with it. I know how to talk to White people about some things."

Joni

From my vantage point race conversations are ones we need to have. But sometimes they are hard. Whites can afford not to examine their Whiteness. Some don't identify as White or are colorblind. Your experience reminds me of a defining moment in my life as it concerns race. It was circa 1965 in Minnetonka, and I was eleven years old. My parents and two brothers were eating dinner around the kitchen table while watching our black and white television where civil rights protests and Dr. Martin Luther King were on the nightly news. A house across the street was for sale and as I recall it, my older brother turned to my dad and stated, "If Negroes (in those days Blacks were called Negroes) bought that house, the property value of our house would go down."

I remember my dad getting visibly angry, which was unlike him, and snapping back to my brother, "Don't you ever say that again. I don't care what the property value of this house is. Anyone can buy that house; I don't care who buys it! Don't you ever say that again!" His vehemence and passion cut through me like a knife. I did not understand the concept of property value and racism at the time, but I knew that something really important was being communicated, something that came from deep within his own experience.

You see, your grandfather grew up poor and lost his own dad, John Hlavacek, Jr. (1889–1922) when the young Elmer David was nine. He occasionally told the story of how his dad died in the dead of a Minnesota winter, so they could not bury him in the frozen ground until spring; "your great grandfather's body remained on their home's cold front porch for two months." This was both an eerie and painful time for our dad (D. Hlavacek, personal communication, January 27, 2019).

Dying young was not uncommon at the time. John died of some sort of throat infection or tonsillitis, four short years following the flu pandemic that hit Minnesota and the world in 1918. Young adults died quickly right along with children and the elderly (National Archives and Records Administration, 2009). The young Elmer David would soon have to take over the family farm in Minnetonka when he was but a child. He was acquainted with grief.

How is it that a White man who never lived around Blacks, had no Black friends, or never directly entered into the Black experience in America in the first half of the 20th century had any understanding of this experience, much less the ability to express it in such a way to so strongly impact his daughter? This kitchen table conversation marked me for life—later I went back to my brothers and mom and asked them if they remembered it—and no one did. The moment was designed for me and defined my future in many ways.

Rebecca

I grew up around White people, and I know their minds sometimes. From my experience, communicating with Whites has to be organic. For me it is. You meet people, you are friendly, and it is natural. I am not completely 100% comfortable with who I am; I want a nose job, a bigger butt, and to lose weight. But I don't feel uncomfortable or weird like I stand out, and I feel comfortable with all groups. Maybe because I grew up around White people. I don't know what it is, Mom, seriously.

Speaking of defining moments, one that gave me insight into White people was in Minnesota, in a relative's kitchen snacking on a bowl of mixed nuts. Grandma was in her 90s at the time. We sat so close that our arms touched. As I recall it, Grandma picked up a Brazil nut and quizzically turned it over in her hand and said, "Nigger Toe, huh, Nigger Toe." She said it so easily like "wow, I haven't seen this in a long time"—recalling the past somehow. I am quite sure she didn't realize that she was saying a racist slur, or that I was any different than anyone else in the family; I was part of the circle. My aunt and uncle tried to tell her, "No, Mom that is a Brazil nut," and they both looked noticeably uncomfortable.

I felt like I was in the Twilight Zone, so I started laughing out of sheer incredulity and the fact that Grandma didn't put two and two together. It was so bizarre. But it wasn't talked about, or explained, or unpacked. We just moved on. But the experience provided me with insight. I was an insider, but I thought about how White people can talk freely in the privacy of their own homes. They may say things in their homes that they won't say in the outside world.

According to some Whites I am considered an "acceptable" Black like Oprah or Condoleezza Rice; these are socially acceptable Blacks—affluent and accomplished. When in Minnesota, individuals say things like: "you remind me so much of Oprah, or you are doing and becoming so much like Condoleezza Rice, you remind me so much of her." These women are exceptional Blacks and I was one of them—the model minority. I hate that term. I hate that comparison. Race will always apply.

Color Struck

In 1903 DuBois wrote "the problem of the twentieth century is the problem of the color line" (p. 41). However, according to playwright Kim Hines,

DuBois was color struck himself. Today we use the word colorism. Colorism is the distinctions and discrimination based on skin color (light, medium, and dark) which affects individuals' behavior, attitudes and treatment of one another. Colorism can be interracial or intra-racial and is deeply rooted in White supremacy (http://colorismproject.com). Colorism is a form of racism, whether it is light skin privilege or believing dark skin is the pure standard of Blackness (Kendi, 2017).

DuBois was a light-skinned Black and according to Kendi, DuBois did not recognize light skin privilege and the other color line (2017). Marcus Garvey, the Jamaican-born activist, political leader, journalist and orator, following Booker T. Washington's death, confronted and debated DuBois around this issue. Garvey, who was dark skinned, came from another perspective of looking down on light-skinned Blacks as not pure Blacks (Kendi, 2017; Snell, 2017). According to Snell, when examining shades of color, the most viable skin tone economically and socially is "the color of White covered by sun-oriented tan" (2017, p. 208). Hence, the attraction to sunbathing.

Rebecca

Color struck? No. I never heard that term, but I have seen colorism if that is the same thing—light skinned Blacks looking down on darker skinned Blacks. I have seen it with people in Haiti and Africa. You see it in the Caribbean, the lighter skins look down at the darker skins but the darker look at the lighter as superior and elevate the lighter skin. A brown skin person is the standard of beauty. That has been my experience. I do hear "dark skin, light skin"; my friends never talked about it. African Americans in the US tend to be prouder of their Blackness than other places I have been. Non-African Blacks—they like Africans more than White people. In Africa, they elevate White people.

I've always been happy with my color. Never have I felt that "oh, you are dark." I love laying out in the sun. I didn't know that a lot of Black people avoid the sun because I didn't grow up in the Black culture. I have two recollections of this. The first was when I was in Haiti, and we had worship services outside. One day sitting on a shady bench with other Black local staff, the sun gradually started to shine on us as it rose in the sky. I welcomed the sun but everyone else was far away from it back into the shade. My face has always been darker than the rest of my body—more exposed to the sun. So, I would sit in the sun to make the rest of my body uniform with my face. The others found it perplexing and questioned me, "You don't mind being in the sun?"

The second incident was at a Samaritan's Purse staff retreat, the Non-Governmental Organization I worked for in Haiti. There were a few Blacks at the retreat, but most of the staff were White. Most of the Whites were sunbathing at the retreat center beach; others, both Black and White, were doing other things. Some of the Blacks did not wear bathing suits but kept their street clothes on in an attempt to cover their entire bodies. Pastor Pierre, my pastor who I love and respect, was one of them.

I was laying on a beach chair in the sun. Pastor Pierre looked at me and said publicly, "What is she doing? Look at her! What is she doing?" I said, "I'm Sunbathing." He responded, "Sunbathing?! Humph, Humph. Look at her! Humph, sunbathing!" Someone purposely sunbathing to be darker was like a foreign language to him. In his mind and others, Black people do not sunbathe. Black people don't want to be darker. I realized that he had never heard of someone purposely trying to be darker. I don't know if he thought that I thought I was White. But everyone knew I was adopted by a White family. Then after being in Africa and Haiti, I saw that colorism is a real thing, and Black people don't want to be darker; some are even bleaching their skin to be lighter.

Joni

I have always liked sunbathing, and I guess I am the one responsible for introducing you to it. I revel in the warmth of the sun at the beach and vitamin D. If truth be told, I also like the tanned look of my skin after sunbathing and how it makes me feel and look—healthy, outdoorsy. I am intrigued that the most "marketable" color socially and economically is White with a sun-oriented tan—perhaps I have subconsciously understood this because of so many media messages.

But I have never wanted or desired to look Black; I know I am White. So, this idea of cultural appropriation (Blay, 2016) is a new one for me. People lose jobs and rightly so over cultural appropriation—Megan Kelly and Blackface, Elizabeth Warren stating that she has Native American blood, and football teams named the Redskins, Chiefs, are cases in point. Are White women who tan in the sun committing the crime of cultural appropriation by mimicking Black skin? Is tanning any different from lightening or bleaching for Black women? Perhaps Pastor Pierre's strong and emotional reaction to your sunbathing was not so small a matter. I never gave laying in the sun a second thought– now I do. That's not to say I will stop, but I will think more about it when I do. Do we sometimes know too much?

Rebecca

Hmmm, maybe so. I have seen and know a lot of things because God has enabled me to be in a White family and to do international, intercultural, and interracial work. This places me in a unique position of experience. I haven't wanted to do *anything about the racial issues in the US. I have always wanted to work internationally, but it is hard to avoid. I will probably end up marrying someone White, but I want him to be somebody who is talking about racism in a Christian context and to stand with me in solidarity.*

When you are awakened, it is hard to be in an interracial relationship with a White guy, however. White people may not be racist on an individual level, but there is collective White supremacy. That is real. It's hurting many Black people. So those are some of my challenges.

Joni

I agree collective or institutional racism hurts Blacks most, but I think it scars and hurts everyone. As a country we are all scarred by racism and ignorance. But knowing and being awake, as you put it, is not easy.

Rebecca

Yeah, White guys hit on me. That's the thing. But when you are a Black person who understands the system that is holding people down, you need to meet somebody who wants to understand, a package deal and understand that there is White privilege. In 2013, I was with an Italian guy, and we were walking down the street in Harlem. This Black guy on the street was yelled and screamed at us, "How are you with the colonizer, with the slave master?! The White guy I was with was really scared. If looks could kill, we would have been dead. Here he was with this beautiful Black woman, and it was like the guy was saying to me—you should be with us. But I don't meet many Black men who are in my social circles. Some are intimidated by me. It's frickin crazy in this country.

When you are awake to racism and White supremacy, it is a challenge to just say "It doesn't exist so maybe I will marry a White guy. Marry a White man, live in a White neighborhood, have mixed children and deny everything. I could be one of those Black people who say, "you're the problem, pull your pants up." But I cannot do that, I know too much- this is something I am really grappling with. I want to understand, change and challenge White privilege if I were to marry a White man.

Erasure

For two decades the Dakota were poorly and unfairly treated by the Federal government, local traders and settlers in Minnesota. Then they revolted in 1862 during what was called the Dakota Uprising (History.com, 2018), a violent and bloody conflict between European settlers and the Dakotas. Not only did many Dakota and settlers lose their lives, the Dakotas lost their territory and much of their way of life. Shortly after, the federal government began sending Dakota children off to boarding schools for the purpose of assimilation into Euro-Canadian culture. As late as the 1960s and early 70s, there is evidence to suggest that Native American children who left the reservations were kidnapped, in other words child trafficked, for adoption or relocation in boarding schools across the country (K. Hines, personal communication, March 8, 2019). The goal of these boarding schools was ideological, linguistic, emotional and physical erasure of Indian culture through the removal of children from their families and tribes (Emery, 2012).

Despite these atrocities, today four Dakota nations and seven Ojibwe reservations exist, and there are 11 federally recognized tribal nations in Minnesota; sovereign governments who have fought doggedly against erasure to maintain their rich cultures (Minnesota Indian Gaming Association, 2018). Despite attempted erasure of their land, language, culture, Native Americans are citizens of hundreds of sovereign native nations and more than 5 million Native American citizens exist here, some with dual citizenship across the US. There are approximately 70,000 registered Lakota primarily in in the Dakotas, Montana and parts of Canada (Indians.org, 2018).

Rebecca

What is my background? Do we know? So, like I don't know. Because we do not know who my birthparents are? You have to have facts first to erase something. There are no facts for me. If I did a DNA test, it would tell me my African ancestry but not the names of my birthparents, not specifics because we don't know, so there is nothing to erase if there was nothing there to begin with. History and background—you must have concrete facts first.

Joni

No, we do not know who your birthparents are and in a sense that is erased from you. Yet and still, I look at erasure differently. Growing up in Minnetonka both Catholic and public schools, I do not recall ever having studied or discussed Native American cultures specifically Dakota and Ojibwa. The social studies textbooks were centered on European cultures and nations, and then most profoundly with a northern European focus. Eurocentric positionality was endemic to the curriculum in the late 1950s and 60s. Thankfully that has changed somewhat as Minnesota's academic standards, since the early 2000s, now contain language in all content area standards related to American Indian instruction and contributions (K. Oliphant, personal communication, January 23, 2019).

Lake Minnetonka—I will swim in it again but never see it the same; I won't have the freedom of a child. Should we swim in it together- pay homage to Dubois and the Dakota? We will know that Dubois very likely swam in it, grappling with the pain of discrimination; the Dakotas saw it as sacred and filled it with their tears. I may have known there was something sacred about Lake Minnetonka as the Dakota's understood; I certainly understand DuBois floating in the middle of the lake—the freedom, the lightness, the buoyancy—and I understand these are the privileges of being White.

References

Allyn, D. (2015). The Dakota uprising: Lake Minnetonka and Dakota holy ground. *Northern Light: Scholarly Journal of North Hennepin Community College.* http://northernlightnhcc.org/?p=152. Accessed January 7, 2019.

Blay, Z. (March 14, 2016). Should tanning be considered appropriation?" *The Huffington Post: Black Voices* http://huffingtonpost.com/entry/should-tanning-be-considered-appropriation_us_56e6d370e4b065e2e3d678fa. Accessed January 7, 2019.

Deloria, V. & Wildcat, D. R. (2001). *Power and place: Indian education in America.* Golden, Colorado, Fulcrum Publishing.

Dregni, E. (2014). *By the waters of Minnetonka.* Minneapolis: University of Minnesota Press.

DuBois, W. E. B. (1920). *Dark water: Voices from within the veil.* New York: Harcourt, Brace and Howe.

DuBois, W. E. B. (2007). *Dusk of dawn.* New York: Oxford University Press.

DuBois, W. E. B. (1906). *Speech at Harpers Ferry, Virginia.* http://www.elegantbrain.com/academic/department/AandL/AAS/ANNOUNCE/niagaramovement/harpers/harperspeech.html

DuBois, W. E. B., (1903). *The souls of Black folk.* New York: Dover Publications.

Emery, J. (2012) Writing against erasure: Native American students at Hampton Institute and the Periodical Press. *American Periodicals* 22(2), 178–198.

Excelsior-Lake Minnetonka Historical Society. (2019). *A brief history of the south lake Minnetonka area* ... http://excelsior-lakeminnetonkachamber.com/history.html

Hines, K. (2001). *Summer in the shadows.* Minneapolis: Minnesota. Unpublished.

History.com. (2018). *Dakota uprising begins in Minnesota.* http://www.history.com/this-day-in-history/dakota-uprising-begins-in-minnesota

Indians.org. (2018). Lakota *Indians* http://indians.org/articles/lakota-indians.html

Kendi, I. (2017). Colorism as racism: Garvey, DuBois and the color line. *Black perspectives.* http://aaihs.org/colorism-as-racism-garvey-du-bois-and-the-other-color-line/

Meyer, E. W. (2003). *Lake Minnetonka's historic hotels.* Excelsior, MN: Excelsior-Lake Minnetonka Historical Society.

Minnesota Indian Gaming Association. (2018). Minnesota gaming tribes and casinos. https://www.mnindiangamingassoc.com

National Archives. (April 30, 2009). National Archives recalls flu pandemic of 1918. https://www.archives.gov/press-releases/2009/nr09-77.html

Ogland, J. (2001). *Picturing Lake Minnetonka: A postcard history.* St. Paul, MN: Minnesota Historical Society Press.

Play Summer in the Shadows. (October, 2001). American Theatre ISSN: 8750-3255. Unpublished play.

Reicher, M. (2018). Battle of Shakopee, MNOPEDIA. http://www.mnopedia.org/event/battle-shakopee-1858

Snell, J. (2017). Colorism/Neo-Colorism. *Education* 138(2), 205–209.

The Minneapolis Tribune. (July 27–August 4, 1988). By the lake side. https://newspapers.mnhs.org/jsp/viewer.jsp?doc_id=mnhi0031/1DFC6J58/88090101&page_name=1

Unze, D. (2011). *New info on state's earliest inhabitants found in BWCA. MPR News.* https://mprnews.org/story/2011/10/02bwca-research

Upham, W. (2001). *Minnesota place names: A geographical encyclopedia. 3rd edition.* St. Paul, MN: Minnesota Historical Society Press.

Zamir, S. (1995). *Dark voices: W.E.B. Dubois and American thought 1888–1903.* Chicago, IL: The University of Chicago Press.

· 4 ·

CZECH REPUBLIC

"Perhaps somewhere, someplace deep inside your being, you have undergone important changes while you were sad."

Rainer Maria Rilke

Joni

I think there are moments in life that are "done unto you." They happen and may seem inconsequential to others but by Providence, by God, they were ordained. One such moment for me was when I was a child in Sister Mary David's sixth grade class at St. Therese Catholic School in a little hamlet in Minnesota called Deephaven. Hmmm, Deep haven; until this moment I never thought about the name. But yes, this little village tucked away in Minnetonka would prove to be a deep haven.

Sister Mary David was a youngish nun with a beautiful face that was framed by her habit. None of her hair showed. We, children, always wondered if her head was shaved or if she had long, beautiful locks under her headpiece. She was a kind and a good teacher, but mostly I remember her love.

So, the incident that would mark me surely was not done in malice nor was it intentional. Our school day followed a regimented schedule: 8 am—Religion; 9 am—Math; 10 am Social Studies and so forth; every day the same. In social studies, we worked our way methodically through a textbook that was heavy on the cultural studies of Europe and North America and sparse on Africa and South America. This was 1964; ethnocentrism and Eurocentric history was on full display.

To Sister Mary David's credit, she asked each of us to find out about our ancestry (we were all White) and prepare with artifacts a little presentation when "our country of ancestry came up in the textbook." This excited and engaged me, and I looked ahead in the book to find when the day for me to present about Czechoslovakia would be. In this class, I was the only child of Czechoslovakian descent; my parents spoke Czech in the home to each other but never taught me and my siblings. Most of time, they referred to themselves as Bohemians not Czechoslovakians. But generally, they wanted us to be Americans.

My classmates were of mainly Norwegian, Swedish, Dutch, English, French, Irish, or Polish descent; heavy on the Scandinavian—Anderson, Swanson, Johnson, Paulson, Davidson. My last name was Hlavacek. A common Czech name in Europe but not common in Deephaven. The northern and western European countries appeared first in the book with multiple pages on each country describing the history, culture, and languages of each. In contrast, Czechoslovakia had a half to a third of a page devoted to it. At the time it was an Eastern bloc country, poor and marginalized under Communist control; I suspect that is why it occupied so little space in the textbook. Nonetheless, it was there, and I planned to present my country that day. I prepared days before with my artifacts and stories from my parents. The day before "my day", my best friend, Julie Davis, who was Polish, presented. I recall she showed some beautifully crocheted items and pottery from her Polish grandparents. The morning of my presentation I was ready with a little bag of items stashed under my desk that my mom had helped me put together.

At 10 AM on the dot, Sister Mary David said, "Take out your social studies book and turn to page 96." Czechoslovakia was at the bottom of page 96. I was already on the page. I remember vividly that the nun then glanced at page 96 briefly, scanning the page from top to bottom, then what seemed to me in my memory, she forcefully turned the page and went on to another country and another child's presentation. I still remember the bodily sensation of that moment although I would not be able to understand and process it until years later as an adult. It was as if something heavy dropped through my body—like my heart fell.

In those days, as a child you did not raise your hand and tell the teacher "you forgot me, you forgot my country." You couldn't interrupt or comment—and I was also quite a shy child so any thought of letting the teacher know she skipped my country didn't even occur to me. But something happened to me that day that shaped me. In some very small way, I experienced what it must be like to be dismissed, to have *your culture, ethnicity, identity erased and minimized. I later vowed that whenever it was within in my power, I would never do that to anyone else. Ever.*

Rebecca

I spent three months in the Czech Republic as a "missionary." I was in Olomouc, the sixth largest city in the Czech Republic—less than half a million people. My experience was a hard one. I felt that the Czech people were a very hard people, and they didn't smile much. The society seemed depressed as a result of communism's failure, no freedom of expression, no freedom to stand out.

Everything was grey, no colors, a big contrast to Holland and Austria where they decorate, and they have more freedom. Maybe too much. I felt uncomfortable in the Czech Republic. People were always staring at me; there were no Blacks (as in African American or African) although there were ROMA, who are referred to as Black in some areas of Europe like Romania and Bulgaria.

Brief Background of the Czech Republic

The Kingdom of Bohemia is usually considered the precursor to the Czech Republic as we know it today. Established in the 12th Century and surviving until 1918, it became part of the Hapsburg Austro-Hungarian Empire following the dissolution of the Holy Roman Empire in 1806. The Bohemian Kingdom went through the 13th century of growth, the golden age of the 14th century, and the Hussite movement and wars of the 15th century. Bohemia and its capital, Prague, was known through the centuries as an artistic, architectural, and intellectual capital of Europe (CIA and US State Dept., 2019; My Czech Republic, 2019).

In terms of modern history, the Kingdom of Bohemia became Czechoslovakia, an independent nation in 1918 at the end of WWI following the collapse of the Austro-Hungarian Empire. The country struggled to survive through the depression, and did, but in 1938 it was annexed by Hitler to become a German protectorate. At the end of WWII in 1948, and under a complicated set of circumstances, the Communist Party of Czechoslovakia won victory, and with the support and aid of the Soviet Union, communism dominated until the Velvet Revolution of 1989 (Encyclopedia Britannica, 2019).

The Velvet Revolution was a non-violent and bloodless overthrow of the Communist Regime which brought back democracy to Czechoslovakia following over forty years of both Nazi occupation and Communism. The playwright, Vaclav Havel was one of the leaders of the revolution and later became president. Four years after the revolution, the country split into the Czech Republic and Slovakia; termed, the Velvet Divorce. The Czech Republic joined NATO in 1999 and the European Union in 2004. (Shepard, 2000)

Joni

As I look back now, my parents always identified as Bohemians which I now under-stand to be the predecessor of the Republic today. They were truly bi-lingual, but at the time we didn't look at this as an asset but almost a liability that somehow marked us as from another country, not quite American, and maybe a little marginalized.

I now remember being one of the only children in my elementary schools with a name like Hlavacek—or at least, it seemed that way. It was a "foreign" name, somehow different, and the teachers could never pronounce it. Whenever they got to my name in the alphabetical roll call for attendance, I inwardly cringed as the teacher struggled with the pronunciation and the children invariably, laughed. Often male teachers said, "are you related to John Havlick?" who was an NBA Boston Celtic star of Czechoslovakian and Croatian heritage. I was not related.

My parents, it seems to me, preferred the marginalized. My father was the first to teach me about race and racism during our kitchen table conversations. With my mother, I recall her curiosity and appreciation for the Native Americans—some summers we traveled to the reservations in Northern Minnesota and bought Indian items: moccasins, Indian dolls, and beaded jewelry. My mother seemed to see value in the people and their way of life. This is the way I like to remember her. Then there were the Gypsies, as she called them, in the late 1950s in Minnesota. She told me there were Gypsies or ROMA living nearby. I never saw them, but I was always looking out for them. Her mentioning of them left a strange memory in me. Later in life I asked her if we had Gypsy ancestry somewhere in the Hlavacek line and she said, "absolutely not."

The Romani

The ROMA (Romani) people are among Europe's most hated ethnic and racial group. Originally migrants from North Western India sometime between the 6th and 11th centuries, they have long had a presence in the Eastern Europe. They are an extremely heterogeneous conglomerate of ethnic sub-groups belonging to different clans or tribes with no common language or religion (The Economist, 2000, p.62). Formerly and frequently called Gypsies, they are a non-territorial nation connected not through geography but through blood ties, common history, and culture. Eight million ROMA are spread across Europe, particularly in the former Soviet Bloc. The group is also categorized as an *ethnoclass*—(Gurr and Harff, 1994), an ethnic group that resembles a low social class with the need for education, better housing, and employment.

Throughout history, this group underwent persecution, oppression, sterilization of the women, violence, slavery, and extermination at the hands of European peoples and governments. One of many tragic recent examples was in Switzerland between 1926 and 1972 when scores of Romany children were forcibly taken away from their parents for fostering. The ROMA today continue to be outcasts, scapegoats, and refugees (Woods and Blenett, 2019).

In America, it is estimated that about one million diasporic ROMA are assimilated into society. The U.S. census does not identify them as a group since they have neither a nationality nor religion (Webley, 2010), thereby making identification hard and an accurate count, difficult. In the last decade, many have sought asylum and refugee status in the UK and Canada with varying degrees of success (Vermeersch, 2003).

ROMA in the Czech Republic

During World War II, the ROMA, along with Jews, were a main target of Nazi extermination programs, ethnic cleansing, and the subject of forced relocation and other radical social policies during the Communist era. From 1938–1945 in the Czech lands, 90% of Roma were exterminated as Hitler implemented the Final Solution to what the Nazis called the Gypsy Question, how to deal with the ROMA population (Woods and Blenett, 2019).

The Lety Concentration Camp in northern Bohemia is where Czech citizens in collaboration with the Nazis committed genocide; victims were drowned, shot sometimes with their bodies being torn apart by dogs in the presence of children. It is estimated that 1309 people were interned in Lety. Following the war, Lety became a privately owned industrial pig farm, guarded and kept secret by protectorate police and the then Czech government, adding additional tragedy and pain to an already unbearable situation for the 326 survivors (Woods and Blenett, 2019).

In the early 2000s, the Committee for the Redress of the Roma Holocaust advocated for the closing down or relocation of the pig farm in order to properly honor the victims of this ROMA genocide and the public affront to the memory of the victims (Konviser, 2010) Lety became a very powerful symbol in Czech politics of the crimes against the ROMA. Finally, in April of 2018 the pig farm was turned over to the state to become a memorial to the ROMA Holocaust victims. Unfortunately, to this day, Czech right-wing extremists have protested memorialization efforts at the site (Huub, 2008; Romea. cz, 2019).

This history is one of long-standing socio-cultural oppression, human rights violations, and institutionalized racism. As recent as from 1972–1990, many Romany women were coerced into being sterilized (Albert and Szilvasi, 2017) and some ROMA report that life was better under the Communists than in the new republic. In this successor state, challenges remain with respect to education and poverty, and there are frequent tensions with the ethnically Czech majority population over issues including crime and integration. There are a quarter of a million ROMA in the Czech Republic, making up about 2–3% of the Czech population. They are considered a national minority (Gurr and Harff, 1994).

The Romani unemployment rate is 55–60% whereas unemployment in the Czech Republic overall is very low, one of the lowest in Europe. There is a severe lack of affordable housing, and the Romani are segregated into Osadas (ghettos). ROMA children are placed in substandard, segregated and special schools where there are low expectations, few challenges, reduced hours, underfunding and poor facilities. These schools are academically behind normal schools for the majority of Czech children. As a result, most ROMA youth drop out of school by the 9th grade (M. Bruner, personal communication, August 6, 2019).

This substandard education and lack of housing has created an underclass. The cycle continues as employment opportunities continue to be few due to this discrimination and under education. ROMA men look for work in local businesses and the schools, but because of their dark skin they are given few chances.

Like the US where people of color are disproportionately represented in the prison population, ROMA make up 60% of the Czech prison population (50% repeat offenders), yet Romani are only 2.5 % of the population; proportional to their representation in the population, ROMA are 20 times more likely to be imprisoned. Racism is institutionalized and intergenerational (M. Bruner, personal communication, August 6, 2019).

Interracial couples are not accepted and violence against them is per-petrated by Czech Neo Nazis, right wing extremists, and White skin heads. Violent bias crimes are not infrequent and according to one eyewitness to one such racial assault, "he died because he was Black, because he was a Gypsy." In addition, the assailants and murderers frequently are not pros-ecuted for these crimes or given meaningful prison sentences (Woods and Blenett, 2019).

Negative perceptions and stereotypes by Czech nationals toward the ROMA are inbred in the fabric of society. Such stereotypes as "the ROMA are criminals, they steal, they are pathological, they take advantage of the welfare system, and they live in the ghetto. They are noisy, they behave badly, and I hate their dark skin, and they frighten us" are openly expressed by the nation-als. In the words of one Romani, "the Czechs think we are lazy but that is not true—but because of our name, appearance, and accent, [we are not offered jobs]. We want to work; we don't want to take welfare benefits instead we would like to work. [We are] a Black citizen of the Czech Republic, and they are killing us like the Jews." Racism is alive in the Czech Republic (Woods and Blenett, 2019), and the Czechs are among Europe's most racist populations (Stafford and George, 2017).

Rebecca

Where I was in the Czech Republic, racism was a big thing toward the ROMAs. I saw it alive and well there in the way the people talked about them. Yes, I had some contact with the ROMAs, they came to the church. There was one ROMA gentle-man who came, and I remember the church people were really nice to him and tried to help him. ROMAs looked darker than most of the Czechs; like Arabs or Indians that's how they looked, poor, nomadic, Bedouins. They seemed to speak their own ROMA language and broken Czech. I remember there was a homeless guy in the church who reminded me of the same Native Americans in the US; alcoholic, tons of kids, underage parents, not working, marginalized and invisible in the society. I also saw them mostly in central Europe traveling on the bus station especially from Austria Euro lines because it was a cheap way to travel so I saw them frequently— but they were not treated well in Eastern Europe.

I saw the ROMA treated with hatred, blatantly, in their face. As I said, they somehow remind me of Native Americans in the US. They are segregated and dis-proportionally in prison like the US, but somehow as a group they seem different to me from African Americans. African Americans seem somehow more resilient, more hopeful as a group. I saw this all in a short time.

I was only there for a few months, and it was one place where I never learned the language. Czech was a hard language to learn. At first, I went because I thought I might be a missionary. A friend of mine in New York said, "I don't see you as a missionary." But that is why I went there. I thought maybe God was calling me to be a missionary, to work, to preach, and to evangelize. But when I was there, I only preached once and sang once. It wasn't what I thought I would be doing. I made friends.

I don't think I could live there. You must be called to do that kind of work there. I think that maybe the missionaries I stayed with were two people who were probably called. When I was there, I did not see the pastor playing in his band, though I knew he loved music. The missionary situation I was staying in was emotionally toxic.

Joni

You have a strong sense of your core being, your soul, of protecting your soul- a strong sense of self-preservation. That is a sign of an emotionally healthy individual when a person is in toxic environment—a healthy person leaves, changes— unhealthy people stay in the mess.

I understand when you talk about a toxic environment. As a small child, my home sometimes was toxic like that. My mother suffered from mental illness and severe depression. She suffered depression that seemed to get worse as she grew older. It went untreated because in the 1950s and 60s, if you went to a counselor for treatment, you were considered crazy and abnormal. As a child, I remember many nights of arguments and my mom and I crying. I was only a little girl, and my mom was so unhappy so much of the time.

But then she had moments of happiness and peace—mostly when she was reading. She loved books, and she loved quiet time with books. I guess that was her escape from her demons. I would later find escape in books as well. But growing up with a mother who expressed so much emotion and sadness so often, I think influenced me in two ways. First, I learned to be independent; to play outside by myself, to run the neighborhood to escape. Then I learned to not emote, to detach myself from feeling—especially sadness.

But I do not want my mother, your grandmother, to be defined by her mental illness. She was more than her mental illness; it was a part of her for sure, but she was much more. She was the first in her family to graduate from high school. She loved knowledge, and she loved politics—she was a staunch Democrat who loved Hubert Humphrey and President Kennedy. She, and your grandfather who you never met, understood what it meant to be poor and marginalized, and they had a keen interest in different cultures and people groups.

Rebecca

I remember the last time we were with Grandma Hlavacek. You and I were the last people to be with her before she became non-communicative. We were at her nursing home that day to advocate for her care; I remember you were concerned about the attention she was receiving.

That day I tried to detach from my feelings, to detach from the sadness. It was a few days before Christmas in 2014. We were in the emergency room where she had been brought by ambulance from her nursing home. It was sad but when things like that happen I kind of detach myself, so I don't feel the sadness. I tried not to feel anything because I knew something sad was happening. You are in a state of denial, and you say to yourself "wait", this is not supposed to happen.

We had lunch with her at the nursing home before she collapsed, and she started choking on her food. She had trouble eating. I didn't think she was going to die though. She was lucid and participating in a full conversation with us.

She collapsed soon after and the next thing I remember is Grandma was like in a coma of some sort in the emergency room and you and I were with her. But I didn't think she was going to die.

Joni

Me either. Not until I asked the nurse, how is she doing? And the emergency room nurse said, "Not good." Then the doctor came in and said, "She is trying to die." I had never heard such a thing before. But I understood, and I told you that she was dying and that you needed to say what you wanted to say to her immediately.

Rebecca

Yes, I remember that, but I don't remember exactly what I told her. I think I said, "I love you and thank you"; however, I don't remember clearly.

Joni

I recall we both were telling her that we loved her, and I remember she mouthed the words, "I love you." I believe those were her last words. They were not audible because she didn't have the strength, but I am certain she mouthed the words "I love you." And I have always known she did.

Rebecca

OH, *wow. So those were her last words. I didn't think she was going to go. After she died, I remember other family came, and the doctor asked if someone wanted to stay with her and relatives said that you and me would stay. You stayed with her. Yes, and at the funeral I sang, "My chains are gone—Amazing Grace"—with my cousin, Clark. Everyone told me afterward that I could have a second career as a singer. I remember Nathan being really emotional.*

Joni

I also remember Paula's words in her beautiful eulogy—Paula, your cousin, my niece. About the dandelions. She said that as a child she picked dandelions with

Figure 4.1   Rebecca and Grandma Hlavacek

Grandma Hlavacek and that most people look at dandelions as weeds, but Grandma viewed them as flowers and put them in a vase on the dining room table. This is the way I choose to remember her. I also want to look at dandelions as flowers not weeds.

I also choose to remember "that she waited for us" before she died. We had not been to Minnesota on Christmas for over 20 years. This year your father, Paul, suggested that we go. We went. And as I told the story of her death, more than a few people said, "she waited for you to come" so that when we were there, she felt she could leave. I believe that.

We were together when she collapsed, we were together in the emergency room, and this perhaps was ordained, too. I want my last words to you to be "I love you" as well. When your mother leaves you with these last words, they are like precious treasures that shore you up to face the rest of your life with adventure and power; I believe that is why whenever I text you or talk to you or leave you, I want my last words to be "I love you". In case they are my last words. This is not morbid; I just want to shore you up for the journey ahead without me.

References

Albert, G. & Szilvasi, M. (2017). Intersectional discrimination of Romani women forcibly sterilized in the former Czechoslovakia and Czech Republic. *Harvard Health and Human Rights Journal.* https://www.hhrjournal.org/2017/12/intersectional-discrimination-of-romani-women-forcibly-sterilized-in-the-former-czechoslovakia-and-czech-republic/

CIA and US State Department. (2019). *Czech Republic: A brief comprehensive study of Czech Republic.* Washington, DC: CIA.

Encyclopedia Britannica. (2019). Czechoslovakia: Historical nation, Europe. www.britannica.com/place/Czecholslovakia

Gurr, T. & Harff, B. (1994). *Ethnic conflict in world politics.* Boulder, San Francisco, Oxford: Westview Press.

Huub, V. B. (2008). The way out of amnesia? Third text, 2008, 22(3), 373–385, DOI: 10.1080/09528820802204854

Konviser, B. (2010, May 30). Fighting to honor the Roma. Blog https://www.pri.org/stories/2009-05-18/fighting-honor-roma. Accessed January 11, 2019.

My Czech Republic-Czech History. (2019). Blog. www.myczechrepublic.com. Accessed January 11, 2019.

Rilke, R. M. (1992). *Letters to a young poet.* San Rafael, CA: New World Library.

Romea.cz (2019, August 17). Commemoration at WWII-era concentration camp for Roma in Czech Republic to give award for humanity in memoriam to Dr. Alfred Bader. www.romea.cz/en/news/czech/

Romea.cz (2019, August 17). Czech state is now the official owner of the pig farm at Lety on the Romani genocide site. http://www.romea.cz/en/news/czech/czech-state-is-now-the-official-owner-of-the-former-pig-farm-at-lety-on-the-romani-genocide-site

Shepard, R. (2000). *Czechoslovakia: The velvet revolution and beyond.* New York: Palgrave.

Stafford, T., & George, G. (2017). European map of implicit racial bias. Figshare. Figure. http://doi.org/10.15131shef.data.4750588.v1

The Economist. (2000) Are they a nation? *The Economist*, 357(8198), pp. 61–62.

Vermeersch, P. (2003). Ethnic minority identity and movement politics: The case of the Roma in the Czech Republic and Slovakia. *Ethnic and Racial Studies* 26(5): pp. 879–901.

Webley, K. (2010, October 13) Hounded in Europe, Roma in the U.S. keep a low profile. *Time.* http://content.time.com/time/nation/article/0,8599,2025316,00.html. Accessed October 19, 2019.

Woods, B. & Blenett, K. [Retrieved 2019, August 17] (Producers & Directors), You Tube. Gypsies, tramps and thieves (Confronting Racism Documentary) – Real Stories. A True Vision Production for Channel 4 T.V.

· 5 ·

VIENNA, AUSTRIA

"Until lions have their historians, tales of the hunt shall always glorify the hunters."

African Proverb

Rebecca

Vienna was such a special time for me. I really felt it was my full transition into adulthood. After I left the Netherlands and finished working as an au-pair for two years, I got a serious itch to study international relations and eventually work at the UN and live in Europe. I went to the University of Minnesota (U of M) the fall of 2009 for one semester and then participated in their study exchange program in Europe in the Spring of 2010. I was so excited when I received the letter accepting me into the good governance exchange program in Vienna, Austria as well as an internship at the International Atomic Energy Agency, the UN branch established after World War II. This professional internship provided me with valuable work experience and propelled me into the international career I desired.

Joni

I remember that time well; I was happy you were attending my alma mater, the U of M and were near my friends and family. The internship in Vienna was a bonus and fortunately and unfortunately paved the way for me to visit you again.

Rebecca

Although that year was such a special time for me with so many dreams and good things that fell into place for me, it was also a time of severe health issues.

For years, I had heavy menstrual cycles and was constantly dizzy, easily fatigued and didn't know what was wrong. Once I was hospitalized at the U of M for passing out while walking to the campus library. A series of tests, blood work and labs could not find the cause of this chronic problem. While in Austria, as I was walking into my apartment in the 3rd district, I started to feel dizzy. Luckily, I was already inside my apartment, mere feet from my bed.

The same feelings that overtook me at the U of M seized me that day in Vienna. I knew the signs. It was my body screaming, letting me know that I did not have enough iron in my system, and that my hemoglobin was too low for my heart and lungs to continue their support.

The prolonged heavy menses I experienced the previous three weeks left my body drained and my brain screaming for oxygen. I lay down on my bed and waited for my roommate to come home from work. The scene that awaited her was enough for her to call an ambulance. I was in bed lying in a pool of my own menstrual blood and was so weak that I could not move. When the ambulance arrived in true Austrian style—on time and with great efficiency—I was taken to a nearby specialized hospital.

I was quickly whisked to the Intensive Care Unit where I received a series of tests and lab work. Following these procedures, the attending doctor returned, he was accompanied by other doctors who couldn't believe what the tests were reading. They wanted to see me firsthand. My hemoglobin was at 2.5, critically below the normal level of 12.0 to 15.5 grams per deciliter for an adult female.

I was quickly placed in a wheelchair because I was too weak to walk and wheeled from the emergency room to a private room. It was deja vu from the previous year. Then the only thing I remembered was waking up in a hospital room tied to a blood transfusion set. I was told that time that my hemoglobin was critically low at a 3.0, and that is why I passed out.

Joni

I was scared for you. Both times. The first time I couldn't make it to be with you, so I sent an old boyfriend who'd become a pastor to visit you and pray with you in the hospital. The second time I went to Vienna and arrived right after you finished the surgery.

Rebecca

This time, in Vienna, I wasn't as frightened as I was when this first occurred in Minnesota. The experience in Minnesota was the first time I had been hospitalized, so I didn't know what to expect. Also, I was completely alone. Luckily in Austria, I had my roommate who stayed with me every step of the way providing translation from German to English and vice versa. I was just grateful that the root cause was finally found!

A smart female, Indian doctor asked me if I had ever had a sonogram because my problem was clearly gynecological. She asked me if I would consent to a sonogram so that she could determine what was causing the heavy menstrual bleedings which resulted in the anemia. The sonogram revealed two fibroids with one at 6.7 centimeters and another small one that was growing as benign cysts in my uterus. Following this diagnosis, I was assigned to undergo laparoscopic surgery, which entailed small incisions in the abdomen and pelvic regions to remove the fibroids, a week-long hospital stay and a six-month recovery time.

I was so nervous because I was not working at the time and from my experience in America, I knew that the surgery was not going to be cheap. I was studying and doing an internship at the UN, and although I had student insurance, I knew it wasn't going to cover the total cost of the operation.

Universal Health Care

Along with many European countries, Austria is a social welfare state and built on the values of solidarity and equality. Its citizens are required to pay taxes that support universal health care, free higher education, strong labor protections and regulations, and generous welfare programs in areas such as unemployment insurance, retirement pensions, and public housing (Federal Ministry of Labour, 2016).

In Austria 98% of the population has medical insurance. An individual's income will determine fees for health insurance, but health care services are provided to everyone equally. This health insurance includes preventive health care for adults over 19 years old focusing on detection of chronic diseases, primary prevention and health counseling (Brunner- Ziegler, Rieder, Stein, Koppensteiner, Hoffmann and Dorner, 2013),

Vienna offers excellent medical care to all its citizens but also to expatriates. Almost any employee is automatically covered by public and universal health care. Vienna has several dozen hospitals with specialties in different medical fields, many pharmacies and excellent emergency services (internations.org/go/moving-to-Vienna/living). Health care is obligatory in Austria and everyone is required to contribute but is rewarded with one of the best healthcare systems in the world.

The one exception to this otherwise optimistic view of healthcare in Austria is the ROMA. The ROMA people in Europe experience healthcare inequalities both in access and in quality compared to non-ROMA peoples. This can include geographic isolation from quality care, language barriers, lack of information, discrimination, degrading treatment and human rights violations in the delivery of health care (Orton et al. 2019).

Rebecca

My experience in the hospital certainly testified to the excellent universal health care that Vienna provided at the time: private room, attentive doctors and nurses, peace and quiet for healing.

Joni

Yes, your private hospital room in Vienna was far different in cost and accommodations from US hospitals. I recall it was like a quaint hotel room with large windows, plants, and tasteful paintings on the wall. There was room for your visitors to sit comfortably

Reflecting on this experience and others earlier in our relationship you have taught me how to be a mother. As a young mother, I was uncertain and perhaps less nurturing than I could have been. I have regrets about this especially with your oldest brother, Nathan. I guess my mother, because she was frequently depressed, expressed her unhappiness about domestic life and motherhood. Her unhappiness influenced my fierce desire to escape her seeming loathing for domestic life and to have a career along with motherhood.

But you were relentless. You demanded my love from the beginning. Clinging to me in the orphanage, demanding that I engage emotionally, crying out for my attention whatever way you could—holding me, misbehaving, making me laugh, having tantrums, and telling me you loved me you expanded me and made me your mother.

Somehow you were able to take my anxiety around motherhood and draw me in—I am far from a perfect mother, but you were able to make me better with your intense desire for me to be so. So, I was there in Vienna with you; in addition to the surgery, we explored the city together.

In the City of Mozart

Often heralded as the "capital of classical music," Vienna is a magnet for those who consider themselves connoisseurs in concertos and masters of Mozart's music. This city is a wonderful place, both for well-established enthusiasts who will delight in the copious concerts available, and for those who are clueless about the genre who want to open their mind to opera and discover the joys of immersing themselves in a dramatic symphony (The culturetrip.com, 2018).

Although many of the most reputable names that Vienna is often associated with did not originate from Vienna, such as Mozart and Beethoven, the city did home-grow many significant composers, including Johann Strauss I and Franz Schubert. Vienna's love affair with art and music is a passionate and long enduring one. Classical music and Vienna are so closely associated today due to the role of the city being the hub throughout the 19th century. During this period, a steady stream of composers flocked to the center of Europe to establish themselves in the Viennese musical scene. This period in musical history is often referred to as the "Viennese Classical Period" due to the ubiquity of classical music that flourished in the city (The culturetrip.com, 2018).

The Black Mozart

But like so much world history especially as it pertains to People of Color, there is a hidden figure who is considered one of Mozart's fiercest nemesis and is often heralded in the modern age as the "Black Mozart." Joseph Bologne, whose noble title was Chevalier de Saint-Georges, was the son of a brief union between La belle Nanon, a great beauty from the island of Grande-Terre in the French colony of Guadeloupe and the wealthy plantation owner and aristocrat, Monsieur Joseph Bologne in the year 1739 (Smith, 2004). Educated and raised in Paris, he received the kind of education that a rich father could provide. He studied literature, science, music, language and dance. In addition, he was an excellent athlete especially as a fencer, runner, marksman, and horse-back rider. Joseph Bologne was an exceptionally gifted student in all respects, but he particularly showed interest and talent in music (Smith, 2004). Because of his father's position as a gentleman, Bologne was able to enter high society as a gentleman despite his color. There were instances of discrimination, however. One instance was as a young man he was allowed in and then disinvited from the Company of the Musketeers, a prestigious branch of the Royal Household's military because of his race (Smith, 2004). Bologne was accepted into English as well as French society, performing as an accomplished composer, conductor, superb violinist, as well as a champion fencer in London and Paris.

Eleven years older than Mozart, it seems that Saint-Georges was everything Mozart wasn't: exotic, brilliant, established, at ease, popular with the ladies, and close to Marie Antoinette, the last queen of France before the French Revolution (Valentino, 2017). There is reason to believe that Bologne was the inspiration for Mozart's, The Magic Flute's most villainous character (Duchen, J. 2016).

This is not hard to believe as Saint-Georges possessed musical abilities especially his skill with the violin which surpassed anyone of his day. In fact, it is believed by some that Mozart copied note-for-note from a Bologne violin concerto into one of his own pieces (Valentino, 2017). It seems in the racist society of their day; Mozart was jealous of Saint-Georges. But in the end, Bologne would be mostly ignored in the list of notable musicians and composers of that age very probably because of his race (Duchen, 2016).

Rebecca

Music and dance offered me escape as a child in the orphanage. I was attracted to the arts and naturally introspective. I remember sitting by myself and staring into the distance wondering what my life would be like when I grew up. When I look back on those reflections, I realize that this was a mature thing to do for a young girl of six, seven, or eight.

One of my earliest and fondest memories of childhood after the orphanage was watching musicals, especially the Sound of Music! I watched that movie so many times that I knew all the lines of all the songs. When I went to the Netherlands to work as an au pair, it was hard for me not to think that I was trying to recreate a childhood fantasy. When the host family asked me what European cities I most wanted to visit, my response was Vienna and Salzburg, cities where the Sound of Music was filmed. I wanted to stand and sing on the same mountain spots where Maria had sung after she left her career as a nun to become the nanny of seven children and ultimately their mother and wife to Captain von Trapp, their father. I was fascinated by how Maria won over the children's hearts and their father's. She ultimately won them over because of the light and life she brought through the joy of music, and dance which she brought into their lives.

My childhood fantasy was to be a Broadway star; to sing and dance my way through life. However, that never happened because I never singularly focused on that career. Although I could not recreate that mental fantasy, I could, with my own version of Maria, the former nun, seek adventure.

When Maria sang, "what would my days be like, I wonder, what would my future be, I wonder," those words deeply resonated with me because even as a young orphan child, I still wanted to make my mark on this world, grow up to find love, and adventure.

Joni

Although my parents, especially my father, liked to dance and enjoyed music my home, growing up, was silent. Our home was quiet; there was solitude. Solitude which I still love. There was no background music or singing in the home that I can recall. So, you, Rebecca, like your father, Paul, were a contrast. You both loved music and wanted music in the home. And, Rebecca, you are a natural—a terrific dancer, singing came easily; it was refreshing.

Although music and dance never came naturally to me, I am a risk taker. So now in my sixties, I am taking dance classes. I'm not great, but not bad, either. Most importantly, I am facing a fear. I am not certain why I have had fears of dancing— not sure where it came from, but I had anxiety about dancing in public especially if it was a line dance or organized dance. Perhaps because I live in my head so much, the cerebral and the body aren't as connected for me. Now I take West African dance and Afro Haitian dance and am facing that fear—my body feels so good and I feel brave.

Rebecca

Music, namely singing and dancing have always been natural talents. I had numerous opportunities to develop and utilize my singing abilities, especially in church as lead soloist, in high school and at my job at Samaritan's Purse. My dancing abilities were never formally utilized until recently when I was living and working in Uganda. I always prized myself as being someone active, taking care of my weight and staying in shape. However, during my years in the Congo, my lifestyle was unhealthy—eating and drinking late at night and doing minimal exercise. As a result, I gained more weight than ever in my life. I was out of shape.

Then moving to Uganda, I was intentional about reversing this course by eating better, practicing a healthy lifestyle, drinking less alcohol, and staying fit through exercise. I was lucky to live near a hotel that offered gym services with a dance studio that no one ever utilized. I saw opportunity! The studio reminded me of weekly dance classes when I was young. I used what I gained from those classes as a basis to start my own dance classes for women like me who wanted to lose weight and have fun.

The class was an immediate hit with the women but also with the men especially when they saw beautiful women shaking their bottoms. I was proud to utilize an underutilized talent to help others accomplish their goals of becoming better and healthier versions of themselves.

Haiti Connection

Joseph Bologne, Saint-Georges, even though he was an aristocrat, was in sympathy with the French Revolutionaries (1789–1799). As a Black man, the cause of the underprivileged and unequal rights was his fight too. He also hoped that the revolution would effect changes in slavery in his island homes of Guadeloupe and San Domingo. Saint-Georges formed the Legion of Men of Color comprised of freed Negroes from the West Indies who had come to France to offer their services in the Revolutionary Wars. However, because of his background in the aristocracy, he was always under suspicion by the new regime and denounced as a traitor and imprisoned during the Reign of Terror in 1793 (Smith, 2004).

After imprisonment, the end of his military career, the death or exile of many of his friends and economic loss during the Revolution, Saint-Georges returned to the place of his birth and his mother's slavery. He returned to

Saint-Dominque (Haiti) to claim the plantation and property that his father left behind. This was the time of Toussaint L'Ouverture and The Haitian Revolution. Unfortunately, Saint-Georges found his father's property, but it had been looted and burned so he left Haiti and returned to Paris. He later died and is remembered as a remarkably gifted man, full of kindness and benevolence who, because he was Black, has not been given the recognition he is due (Smith, 2004). He never left a biography and so his history is seldom remembered due to a propensity to capture only White narratives. Bologne was a prodigy and musical genius but was not recognized because of his being born the wrong color in the wrong era. Fortunately, since the 1990s, attitudes are changing in Europe according to independent music historian William J. Zick. There are classical musicians and fans who now think Joseph Bologne, Saint-Georges is on par and very much comparable to Mozart (Valentino, 2017).

Rebecca

I just recently visited Austria, ten years after my first stay in 2010. Vienna transformed to a more diverse city with now People of Color walking around its airport and city streets.

Before, the only time I saw Blacks was at the church I attended; Africans congregated at the African Fellowship. There has been an influx of Somali and Ethiopian refugees as well as, more recently, Syrian, Afghani and Iranian refugees. Fortunately, a new Austrian chancellor, Brigitte Bierlein, has been appointed. She is the first woman to have this position. The far-right wing has been defeated for now, so there may be some hope in the future of Austria after all.

Joni

You seem more optimistic than some Viennese citizens who say despite a functioning social security and health care system, great technological capability and being the safest capital city in the world, Vienna harbors racism, narrow-mindedness, and the people generally do not do change well (Katschthaler, 2015). I can't personally speak to this perspective, but it does appear that there has been anti-Muslim racism or anti-religious sentiment recently enough for the mayor of Vienna to have to speak out against it (Kiyagan, 2019). According to one blog I read, "Expats have the hardest time making friends here [Vienna]" (Katschthaler, 2015). But this is not true of you. You make friends and keep friends wherever you go. Black friends, White friends, all races and ethnicities, you remind me somehow of the Black Mozart—so talented, able to traverse with the rich and poor, lover of the niceties of life, and kind. Like what I imagine he was—a border crosser.

References

Brunner- Ziegler, S., Rieder, A., Stein, V., Koppensteiner, R., Hoffmann, K., & Dorner, T. (2013). Predictors of participation in preventive health examinations in Austria. BMC Public Health, 13(1), 1138.

Document: Permission for Mme. George Bologne to take Nanon negresse and Joseph, her son aged 2, to France: Archives departementales del la Gironde; 6B/50.

Duchen, J. (February 7, 2016). Chevalier de Saint-Georges: The man who got under Mozart's skin. Independent. https://www.independent.co.uk/arts-entertainment/classical/features/chevalier-de-saint-georges-the-man-who-got-under-mozarts-skin-a6859191.html

Federal Ministry of Labour, Social Affairs and Consumer Protection. (June 2016). Sozial Ministrium. Vienna: Social Affairs Ministry. www/sozialministerium.at/broschhurenservice

Katschtaler, A. (November 1, 2015) Of racism and other things: Why I'll gladly leave Vienna behind (as soon as possible). https://medium.com/@thegrumpygirl/why-i-ll-gladly-leave-vienna-behind-6cd6bac540f6 accessed Febrary 15, 2018.

Kiyaganm A. (May 15, 2019). Vienna mayor condemns racism, anti-religious sentiment. Anadolu Agency. https://www.aa.com.tr/en/europe/vienna-mayor-condemns-racism-anti-religious-sentiment/1478436

Orton, L., Anderson de Cuevas, R., Stojanovski, K., Gamella, J.F., Greenfields, M., La Parra, D., Marcu, O., Matras, Y., Donert, C., Frost, D., Robinson, J., Rosenhaft, E., Salway, S., Sheard, S., Such, E., Taylor-Robinson, D. and Whitehead, M. (2019), "Roma populations and health inequalities: a new perspective", International Journal of Human Rights in Healthcare, 12(5), 319–327. https://doi.org/10.1108/IJHRH-01-2019-0004

The culturetrip.com. 2018. Theculturetrip.com/Europe/Austria/articles/why-vienna-is-a-major-destination-for-classical-music-lovers/

Smith, W. (2004). The Black Mozart: LeChevalier De Saint-Georges. Bloomington, IN: Author House.

Valentino, A. (April 12, 2017). The 'Black Mozart' was so much more. Atlas Obscura. https://www.atlasobscura.com/articles/joseph-bologne-Black-mozart

· 6 ·

PORT-AU-PRINCE, HAITI

"To all my sisters and brothers who have struggled for the liberation of our peoples in the name of Jesus Christ against the heaviest of odds—against the intransigent forces of guns and of miters and of money."

Jean-Bertrand Aristide

1990 was an important year in our lives and an important year for Haiti—the year of its second independence, the democratic election of Jean-Bertrand Aristide by popular free vote on December 16. Rebecca was adopted and left the country on October 11, 1990, just two months before the election, and four months before Aristide was officially sworn in as President on February 7, 1991 as the first democratically elected president in Haitian history. Aristide is a well-educated Catholic scholar and teacher who speaks multiple languages and who has spent time in the US, Canada, Israel and Europe. He is most identified, however, as an anti-Duvalier parish priest who loves the poor of Haiti and, in fact, grew up among the poor. He was elected by the poor masses of Haitians with 67% of the vote with 3.2 million Haitians registered and 2.4 million voting (Sprague, 2012, p. 5). His main support came from a grassroots movement with roots in Haiti's countryside Catholic churches. This movement is called Lavalas which means "the flood" in Haitian Kreyol.

As this monumental event was occurring in Haiti, Rebecca was on her way to becoming an American citizen with a Haitian adoption, and adjusting to school, her two new brothers and life in the US; and Joni was adjusting to becoming a mother of a ten year old girl. We were oblivious to the tide of historical events occurring and only now think back to that time and how the approaching election perhaps precipitated Rebecca's exodus from the island.

Leaving Haiti—1990

Joni

I remember receiving a phone call from the orphanage while I was at work, and the orphanage worker saying that Rebecca was upset and crying thinking that we were not going to come and get her. I was distressed as I already felt I was her mother. We later found out that she had been disappointed before when another American couple said they intended to adopt her and had not returned to do so. Rebecca was devastated by all the delays and the possibility that she would not be adopted. My husband, Paul, and I had been trying for months to have the Haitian adoption approved and ratified by the Haitian courts through an orphanage lawyer. All our paperwork had been completed—home study, fingerprinting, applications, forms upon forms, birth certificates, financial reports, reference letters, etc.—for some time; these mounds of papers were initially in English and then were translated into French. At the time there were no digital copies possible, so we had hundreds of papers. We and our Haitian lawyer, Pastor Luke, could not get the courts to move to finalize our paperwork. Now I am thinking the impending election and turmoil in the country perhaps explains the massive delay—but then again, Haiti has always had a disorganized and chaotic, not to mention corrupt, way of handling its business.

But for whatever reasons, we were unable to complete the Haitian adoption and take her to her new home in the US. This traumatized Rebecca and alarmed me and her father. After receiving a phone call from the orphanage saying Rebecca was extremely upset and thought we were not coming for her, I prayed with a woman from my church and called the American Embassy in Port-au-Prince. From New York. I explained to the individual on the telephone our dilemma about getting the Haitian adoption ratified and all the long delays and Rebecca's despair. I was told to come to the American Embassy in Port-au-Prince and bring all paperwork and that we would receive a "provisionary visa" with which I could bring her to New York and finish the adoption from the US.

I jumped on an American Airlines plane, the only carrier at the time that flew to Haiti, and promptly went with an orphanage translator and missionary, and little

Rebecca to the American Embassy. With the tall stacks of paperwork in hand, the three of us went to the embassy window. Placing the stacks on the sill in front of the consulate, I explained my phone call, the situation in brief and that I had come for the "provisionary visa." The gentleman speaking in English looked at me and said "What is a provisionary visa? I have never heard of it." My heart sank as I looked down at Rebecca hoping she did not understand the gravity of the situation. The missionary, Rebecca and I held hands and prayed, begging God to help us. We were at the mercy of the authorities. After what seemed like an eternity, the consulate came back to the window, and stamped our paperwork "permanent visa." I already knew enough about the international adoption process to know that we were not supposed to be granted a permanent visa without a completed and court-approved Haitian adoption. I took the paperwork, and we hurried back to the orphanage. I wanted to get out of Haiti with Rebecca before anyone changed their mind.

Rebecca

I do not clearly remember any of the happenings in the American Embassy. All I remember is that I wanted to leave and was ready to leave and do something else. The morning we were to go to the airport, I sat in the van ready to go waiting for my new mother; I had already said my good-byes. I looked straight forward and have almost never looked back.

My mom tells me these stories, but these are her stories—the stories of bringing the paperwork to the embassy, Dr. Luke, and the courts. We were children; nobody told us anything about the process of adoption. I do not remember. Or maybe I have chosen not to remember. I am not sure. At nine almost ten, I wanted to leave Haiti, the orphanage and was ready for something else. I wanted to leave Haiti and the orphanage.

We left behind a Haiti bracing for more turmoil. Titid, as Aristide was affectionately called by the poor throughout the country who elected him in UN and internationally supervised fair and free elections continued to be the target of coups and repeated assassination attempts. He survived these multiple attempts on his life and several US backed coups while serving as Haiti's president in 1991, 1994–96, and then again from 2001–2004. In brief, since Haiti's first independence in 1804, Haiti was marked by corruption and dictatorships backed by mainly US and French who did not want to see the Black Republic succeed; the country existed as a "disguised colonialism" (Sprague, 2012; Aristide, 1993). An elite thirty or so families, along with another 200 less elite but still wealthy Haitians with the support of the US, continually worked to undermine, violently resist, economically disable, media smear,

and terrorize, torture and kill through paramilitary attacks anyone supporting President Aristide throughout his years as president. Aristide himself
narrowly escaped assassination on numerous occasions. Furthermore, there is
strong evidence to prove that this violent opposition to Aristide's democracy
was backed economically and politically, with the sanction and support of the
US government, France, and the Dominican Republic in collaboration with
the elite classes of Haitian society previously in power during the years of
Duvalier (Sprague, 2012). Despite this opposition the poor masses of Haitian
society supported Aristide and re-elected him although both international
and Haitian media said otherwise or be silent about what strong support he
had (Chomsky, Farmer, and Goodman, 2004).

One of the most memorable attacks on his life and the popular movement was prior to his first election in 1988. Aristide's parish church, St. Jean
Bosco, was attacked by anti-democratic and anti-Lavalas paramilitary groups
while Aristide said mass. 13 of his parishioners died and 70 were injured in
the attack. Aristide somehow survived (Sprague, 2012; Aristide, 1993;1997).

Our Heads in the Sand

Rebecca

*Growing up I knew nothing about what was happening in my country, about
Aristide; I was kept in an American orphanage bubble—away from the turmoil but
also away from my history and my culture, too. Much later I was told by a Haitian
pastor, Pastor Pierre, who now works at the American Embassy in Port-au-Prince
and who I admire, that Aristide practiced Voodou and was bad for Haiti. And
according to what I heard from some Haitian friends, Haiti was more stable and, in
some ways, better under Duvalier. This is what I heard. I do not know much about
him. I wasn't taught Haitian history in the orphanage and didn't learn it when I came
to the US. One of many reasons I wanted to go back to Haiti was to learn about my
Haitian history and my culture and heritage.*

Joni

*I am mad at myself. Mad because I had my head in the sand and was not aware
of what was going on in Haiti when Rebecca was adopted. If I had been, I would
have understood why all the paperwork was taking so long; I would have been better informed to teach my daughter and her brothers about the historic dynamics*

occurring in Haiti. I feel now as if I somehow robbed her of her history and robbed our family of an appreciation of the strength and resiliency of the Haitian people. I would have also understood the evils behind much of the decades of American involvement in Haiti and the deficit narrative still present today.

We feel humbled to read Aristides's words in the opening of his book, In the Parish of the Poor, (1997) to find Aristide has used the metaphor of birthing and a story of a poor woman about to give birth but needing the solidarity of Haitian bystanders to transport her to the hospital to safely deliver (pg. 4). We adopted this same metaphor for our relationship and one perceptive reviewer for this book noted that perhaps we were presumptuous to compare the birth of Haiti with the birthing of our relationship. Perhaps we are, but somehow birthing and dying are so present in Haiti—with Aristide and 1990 and the success of free elections. This emerging democracy was another Haitian birthing, and in our relationship, we have many birthings and development as mother and daughter.

Aristide is back in Haiti and has just survived another assassination attempt in 2017, he appears to still be widely popular with the masses (Wochit, 2017). What the government has always feared and now fears with President Moises is not violence but peaceful protest by the masses of poor that the government cannot demonize and use to deflect from its own corruption and lack of accountability—that has always been the case. (http://cepr.net/blogs/haiti-relief-and-reconstruction-watch/).

Aristide—the US and the Church

Aristide was a Roman Catholic priest of the Salesian order, a liberation theologian, and vocal advocate for Haiti's poor, oppressed and disenfranchised. In 1985, Aristide became a parish priest at St. Jean Bosco which under his leadership became a center for the mobilization of the poor masses of Haitians in opposition to the brutal Duvalier dictatorship and the widespread corruption and oppression of the Haitian people by elite Haitians in power. It is worth repeating that a small group of elite and upper-class Haitian families oppress and terrorize (Sprague, 2012) the poor of Haiti with the support of American and Dominican Republic paramilitary groups. This elite class essentially keeps the poor oppressed, unequal, and marginalized to this day.

The Catholic Church hierarchy in Rome and Aristide's Salesian order became increasingly uncomfortable with Aristide's political activities. Aristide and his church understood it as their responsibility as Christians and an outgrowth of their faith particularly as understood through Liberation Theology (Boff,1978; Boff, & Boff, 1998). Contrary to popular propaganda in the US, Aristide is, and was, a Christian, not a Voodou priest—as falsely portrayed by media and government officials. Because of his work with the poor in solidarity with anti-Duvalier supporters, the Salesians expelled him and in 1994, Aristide left the priesthood and in 1996 married an American of Haitian descent, Mildred Trouillot.

To this day, the American Evangelical church promotes the predominant narrative that Haiti is a Voodou country and that a conversion to Christianity is the answer to all issues of poverty and oppression. This narrative parallels the "shithole" narrative that has been put forward by the American administration. However, Haiti is predominantly a Christian country and primarily Roman Catholic. According to the Pew Center for Research (2010), 56.8% of the population is Catholic; 29.6% Protestant. Voodou draws on the West African and indigenous Taino traditions. Perhaps Aristide has been erroneously called a Voodou priest because while promoting democracy in his office as President, he recognized Voodou in 2003 as he legalized and sanctioned freedom of religion for all religions including Voodou (Umoja, A., 2011). While Aristide is a Christian, his liberation theology sought to bring unity and engage all Haitians in building the country together in mutual respect. Many Haitians are Catholic but participate and honor the Voodou tradition in the country as part of their heritage and identity (Umoja, A., 2011). Aristide was both misrepresented and misunderstood as he attempted to include freedom of religion as a part of his democratic platform.

Along with this deficit narrative of Haiti and its people as devil worshippers, ignorant and dependent, there is widespread evidence to support the idea that volunteers, missionaries, and aid, in general to Haiti have unknowingly undermined the local economy and businesses (Mauren and Fitzgerald, 2014). A case in point is food aid from the US which for decades (and particularly after the earthquake) has undermined Haitian farmers, particularly rice and corn farmers. According to former President Bill Clinton, "since 1981, the US has followed a policy . . . that we rich countries that produce a lot of food should sell it to poor countries and relieve them of the burden of producing their own food . . .; it has not worked. It may be good for American farmers, but it has not worked [for Haiti]" (Kusher, 2012). Aristide tried to change all of this but was undermined at almost every turn.

Rebecca

My perspective from now working in Africa is that in Africa as well as Haiti there is a great deal of paternalism. Haiti is symbolic of this in so many ways—the first

Black Revolution, slaves defeating one of the most powerful countries in the world and Napoleon. Haiti has been paying for this slave revolution ever since. Haiti's independence has consistently been undermined. From how the US and international media uses propaganda with "let's save Haiti campaigns", to continued government corruption backed by the US, and just sidelining the country at all cost. It all started with Haiti, and they have been paying for it ever since now being the capital of NGO's in the world. But God hasn't forgotten Haiti, and it has the chance to awaken other Black countries, so the same thing does not happen.

It has been a dream of mine since childhood to work internationally and do humanitarian work, but my perception of the way to do this is changing. Aid and assistance are not the way. Foreign assistance is not the way to help Black countries break free. My dream is to help Black nations break free from colonialism in the mind. I am passionate about Black countries being left alone.

"Real" Orphans

According to a report from the Lumos Foundation, 30,000 Haitian children live in privately run orphanages in Haiti. More than a third of the 752 orphanages are funded by US donations. However, an estimated 80% of these children are not really orphaned—meaning they have one or more living parent and almost all have other relatives, according to the Haitian government (Lumos, 2017). Parents through the decades have brought their children to orphanages because they could not feed or educate their children and had hopes that placing them in an orphanage would give them a better life. It seems this was a common practice. Matters were made worse with the earthquake of January 12, 2010. Due to the destruction of Haiti's capital an international call was made to "take care of the children" spawning international quick adoptions, inappropriately handled and circumventing existing safeguards. It was not uncommon at the time for visa requirements for children in the process of being adopted by Americans to be lifted. In some cases, this may have been beneficial; but generally, there was bedlam in the international adoption process. How this affected the welfare of Haitian children overall is still unknown (Gray, 2010).

Rebecca

Sometimes I wonder about my birth parents, especially when undergoing a physical examination and questions of family medical history are asked. But beyond the biological, were my birth parents like other than Black Haitians? I do not wonder or think about that very much. No. I have been living my life and moved on. The only time I wonder is when I have health issues or go to the doctor as I said. I have had a few chronic medical issues, and I wonder then about my birth parents' medical history. Then it would be helpful to know. Otherwise, I have not, and I do not have any longing to meet them, even if it were possible. That door is closed.

Joni

I was told Rebecca's birth mother died in childbirth due to malnutrition and the father was nowhere to be located and that Rebecca was taken directly from the hospital. Is this true? It is the account I was told. So, I have every reason to believe that Rebecca was a true orphan, if you will. I was told several months before the adoption was completed that a notice was placed in a Haitian newspaper asking anyone related to Rebecca to come forward or else the adoption would be finalized. No one came forward to claim her. I never wondered much about her birth parents; however, lately after reading much more about Haiti's courageous history and the Aristide years I have wondered more. I'd like to believe that they were part of the Lavalas grassroots liberation movement with strong faith and strong convictions for the democratization of Haiti under Aristide. I have no way of knowing that this is true.

Rebecca is so strong, so courageous, so civically involved; her character makes me imagine that this could be so. But she is mine. I do remember, however, one little girl who came to the orphanage for the first time when we were there. I recall the staff telling me she had family, but they couldn't take care of her, so they wanted her to be adopted. Now I see this was common. How ignorant I was.

Haitian Orphanages and Faith-Based Organizations

An amazing 90% of the $100 million funding to orphanages in Haiti comes from faith-based organizations in the US. This is seemingly incredibly generous—and it would be if orphanage-based care were in the best interest of children (Lumos, 2017). According to this same report, Haitian children face a range of neglect and abuses of human rights violations in orphanage care. Money would be better spent on keeping children with their families—since it appears many have family members, or adoption into families as a last and careful resort. The Lumos report goes on to recommend that the 100 million dollars donated to orphanages which many times are unsafe spaces and dens for potential child trafficking and abuse, would be better redirected to community-based education, health care, nutrition and family reunification programs (2017).

Haiti ranks eighth in the world for modern day slavery according to the 2016 Global Slavery Index. Haiti's government is non-compliant in meeting the minimum standards to combat child trafficking (Walk Free Foundation, 2016). In terms of child separation, poor families will place their children in wealthy homes to do domestic work; this is commonly known as *restavek*. (Schwartz, R., 2013). But according to a UNICEF 2016 report, 70% of these children are subjected to harsh child labor and sometimes child trafficking. Research overwhelmingly affirms that institutionalization is not best for children; families are. The US moved away from caring for children in orphanages at the turn of the 20th Century and European and New Zealand abandoned orphanages for family support in the 1950s, but Haiti still institutionalizes widely even though it is known that institutionalization of children is harmful for a variety of reasons including: mental and physical developmental delays, exposure to abuse, potential child trafficking, and risk of neglect. Now there are continued questions around orphanages and children's human rights especially with a 150% -increase in orphanages since the Haitian earthquake of 2010. Concern surrounds the inability to track and account for funding support and the limited oversight and supervision of orphanages (Lumos report, 2017).

Haitian Orphanages—Big Business

How can this be? How can it be that well-meaning individuals who genuinely want to help are undermining the economic, familial, and social structures of Haiti? It is a paradox that the Christian community and people of faith have been and are complicit in the oppression in Haiti. There is no doubt that people of faith, and some in the priesthood—liberation theology activist, primarily—have devoted their lives to the poor and oppressed of Haiti and other Latin American countries; Oscar Romero, the martyred priest in El Salvador is a case in point. Aristide, himself is a Christian (Kieser, E. 1989). Others like Eleanor Workman, a Pentecostal Christian, the founder of Christian Haitian Outreach (CHO), the orphanage that Rebecca came from, worked tirelessly for the poor in Haiti as well.

Rebecca

My parents and I went back to the orphanage, CHO, around the summer of 2014. The orphanage looked the same from the outside surrounded by a large concrete barrier fence. It had new management, however. We explained to the guards and those in charge that I had come from CHO and been adopted and that we wanted to go inside just to remember. But they wouldn't let us in. I was disappointed that we couldn't go inside to see it, remember it. But then I took this as a symbol to mean that life had changed, and some answers I would never have and that I need to be ok with that. It is like another time in my life before I went to Jordan and after Haiti, I walked around Valley Stream Park near our second house that had just been sold, and went to all the places we use to go: the coffee shop, SipThis, the old church—I felt the same symbolic thing, a kind of letting go, this chapter was over. The doors of that old home were closed just like the gates of the orphanage were closed. Some answers you may have been looking for may never be found, and I should be ok with that. It's over, good-bye. It was a little hard to do. That chapter of my life is over. My mom said there was a young man at the gate to the orphanage that she remembered as one of the orphans when I was a child. She asked him if he remembered her, but he said no. But then he said, "But I do remember her" and pointed to me. I don't remember this or him. I have no survivor's guilt. No one wants to see people suffering. I feel that that boy was not able to be adopted and I was—I feel bad.

Returning to Haiti

Aristide returned to Haiti as a civilian in February 2011 from exile in South Africa following an election that barred the Fanmi Lavalas party from participating. Post exile, Aristide abstained from political involvement, but despite his inactivity, in 2014 he was ordered under house arrest while a corruption investigation was underway. Lawyers for Aristide and supporters of Fanmi Lavalas protested this illegal judicial action by the government. (Archibold, 2014) He now lives with his wife and children near the US Embassy and keeps a low profile but still retains some popularity with the Haitian masses. Unfortunately, there have still been attempts on his life. (Wochit News, 2017).

Rebecca

The first time I came back to Haiti after being adopted was over twenty years later. I returned with a Christian non-profit organization called Samaritan's Purse. I had a master's degree in International Relations and was now a program director for several social services programs in Haiti—water purifications, health and wellness, and recycling. My mom visited me on several occasions, and we returned to CHO where I spent my first nine years.

It was nice going back. In some ways I didn't feel so connected; I was an expatriate (expat) had an education, had spent so many years in the US. This separated me from the Haitians because of class, experiences, and education. But one thing I noticed we had in common was kindred laugh—we laughed at the same things. We found the same things funny.

Sometimes I was sensitive to the way the American and other international workers treated the Haitians; I saw certain injustices happening and I wasn't going to tolerate it. For example, not too long ago at the NGO where I worked, there was a Haitian line and a White line for the food as if we were in colonialism. And the Haitian staff was treated badly. Comments made about the Haitian people were derrogatory and condescending. I felt a certain sense of solidarity and protectiveness; I could stand up for them when I had a voice and they didn't. And I did.

Joni

I love Haiti. I love the people, the lush vegetation, the spirit of protest, the ocean, and the sky. Remembering Rebecca worshipping in Creole was a highlight for me. Swimming in the ocean was another highlight. I remember swimming in the ocean alone; some workers would not swim because they said the Haitian's bathed and washed their clothes in the sea, but I figured the ocean is huge—I took the risk and am no worse for the plunge.

The best memory I have of that trip in 2014 was Rebecca's struggling to speak in Creole. Even though she delved in deeply with the language, she had lost most of the language when she came to the US in 1990. We had Haitian neighbors and friends, and we had considered putting her in a bi-lingual school with other Haitian immigrant children, but she didn't want to. She wanted to speak English and resisted speaking Creole or associating with Haitians in our neighborhood in Brooklyn, where there was a substantial Haitian diasporic population. She wanted to be an American and soaked in the good, the bad, and the ugly of American culture. But in 2014, Rebecca sang in Creole as she led worship with the Haitian workers at the Samaritan Purse outpost.

Faith Confronted with Oppression

Rebecca worked with Samaritan's Purse, a US Christian and humanitarian organization founded and headed by Franklin Graham, the late Billy

Graham's son. Franklin spoke at President Trump's inauguration and appears to have close ties with this administration. But this organization is only one of hundreds of churches and Christian organizations who along with the UN and other large secular, humanitarian international organizations have built homes, provided clean water and sanitation, taken care of the sick, and cared for orphans (Jackley, 2017), but the question remains "at what cost?." "Haiti is the first Black republic in the world and since its independence in 1804 it has paid a tremendous price for that honor. The payment has been in the form of isolationism from its neighbors in Latin America and the Caribbean; being the first third-world debtor nation to France; experiencing the control of civilian or military dictatorships propped up by the US and the Dominican Republic, having its labor force heavily exploited, its economy devalued, the undermining and oppression of its fledgling democracy movements, and violence done to those who spoke out in the media both in Haiti and in the diaspora. (Wilentz, 1997).

Is the cost the undermining of local economy, support of oppressive dictatorships and elite classes, separation of Haitian families, inadvertent support for the paramilitary which has traumatized a nation for decades, and solidifying institutional racist and colorist structures? Very likely this is true. Where does our faith come down in the midst of oppression of which our own country and organizations are complicit? How do we maintain a thinking and thought-out faith? (Boff and Boff, 1998).

Rebecca

I am a Christian. I love God. But as I examine my faith and my work in Haiti, I think churches and NGO's have helped create a system of dependency and made the Haitian government insecure by relying on outside intervention, knowledge--decades of never being independent from NGOs. Under Duvalier there were many negative things, but to hear some people talk there were more positive things under Duvalier. Some Haitians think a dictatorship is needed—a benevolent dictatorship, that's what they need.

Haiti has become a dumping ground for US garbage—used clothing and surplus food. Haiti is America's garbage can. I am so sick of seeing Americans, especially American missionary groups with t-shirts that say: "Saving Haiti" and "God loves Haiti, too"—White people wearing these stupid shirts.

I don't think White Americans should be in developing countries because they are often racist. Many of them, especially with Samaritans Purse, are, I perceive—never attempting to learn the language Creole, staying in the gated compounds, eating American food, and generally separating themselves from the people. Why are they there? What selfish interest is it serving?

Then again, there is racism, or in the case of Haiti and other parts of the Caribbean, there is colorism and classicism. There is a distinction between colorism and racism. Colorism is discrimination based on skin tone within a particular race but is also a preference for proximity to Whiteness. And in Haiti the ruling power mulatto groups typify the colorism and classicism in Haitian society and manifest themselves like racists in the US.

Joni

I share Rebecca's faith. Rebecca's father and I adopted Rebecca because we believed, and still do, that God directed us to. We were and are Christians but at the time were steeped in an erroneous, ignorant view of Haiti that discounted any understanding

Figure 6.1   Return to Haiti-Samaritan's Purse

of historical context, colonialism, American interference, and the crimes against Haiti committed since before the slave rebellion that created the first Black Republic. Our ignorance although not willful is and was a sin. Having said this, adopting Rebecca is one of the greatest gifts of my life; there are no regrets—I do think it was God's directing. I understand now that adoptions shouldn't be necessary; that children are orphans because of the oppression, racism, and institutionalized destruction of Haitian society within and without. Yet and still, Rebecca is my daughter—I love her with my whole being. Having said this I am deeply troubled by the seemingly mounting evidence that the Christian community is somehow complicit in the oppression that is Haiti, if only complicit by ignorance and doing harm in the guise of good, however well meaning. I have a great deal of respect for Liberation Theology, a movement within Christian theology that in addition to personal salvation emphasizes social, political, and economic liberation for social justice. Liberation Theology was initially developed by Latin American Catholics in response to oppressive regimes and poverty. I lean in that direction in terms of how I process my faith in an oppressive world.

Rebecca

"Haiti, the first independent Black republic in the world, has long been the target of racism. In many ways, anti-Haitian sentiment can be equated with anti-Blackness" (Jean-Charles, 2018). I agree with this statement, and I am passionate about being a part of change. Maybe that is the reason why I was born in Haiti, to help Black people unite. Africans don't know about the diaspora; African Americans who are affluent need to unite so foreign White aid is not necessary. There are many Haitian Americans living in the US and they need to help Haiti and Africa. Black people training Black people, professional people; Black churches instead of White churches. Haitians need to see wealthy Black people; this will revolutionize Haiti and Africa, boasting the economies, vacationing there. Now there are just so many White people in these countries, all the people know is White help. Black Americans have a responsibility. An example of this is the orphanage I came from in Haiti. It made a really big difference that Mom Workman was Black; she was one of us, and it gave us hope. It's revolutionary if Black professionals—engineers building the infrastructure, doctors bolstering and modernizing healthcare—come to Africa and Haiti and unite with the people; not to exploit them.

References

Archibold, R. (September 12, 2014). Ex-President of Haiti put under house arrest. The New York Times. https://www.nytimes.com/2014/09/13/world/americas/aristide-haiti-house-arrest.html

Aristide, J. B. (1997). In the parish of the poor: Writings from Haiti. 9th Edition. Maryknoll, NY: Orbis Books.

Aristide, J. (1993). Jean-Bertrand Aristide: An autobiography. Maryknoll, NY: Orbis Books.

Aristide, J. B. (2000). Eyes of the heart: Seeking a path for the poor in the age of globalization. Monroe, ME: Common Courage Press.

Boff, L. (1978). Jesus Christ liberator: A critical Christology for our time. Maryknoll, NY: Orbis Books.

Boff, L. & Boff, C. (1998). Introducing liberation theology. Maryknoll, New York: Orbis Books.

Chomsky, N., Farmer, P., & Goodman, A. (2004). Getting Haiti right this time: The US and the coup. Monroe, ME: Common Courage Press.

Gray, M. (January 16, 2010). Orphanage: Adoption plan needed for Haitian children. CNN Haiti Earthquake coverage. Haiti: Relief and Reconstruction Watch Blog www.cnn.com/2010/WORLD/americas/01/15/haiti.orphanage/index.html

Jackley, A. (April 19, 2017). What Christians are really doing in Haiti. CNN Opinion/Political Op-Eds/Social Commentary https://www.cnn.com/2017/03/17/opinions/believer-haiti-christian-missionaries-jackey/index.html

Jean-Charles, R. M. (January 12, 2018). I am part of the Haitian diaspora—here's why I wasn't surprised by Trump's comments. America—the Jesuit Review. https://www.americamagazine.org/politics-society/2018/01/12/i-am-part-haitian-diaspora-heres-why-i-wasnt-surprised-trumps-comments

Kieser, E. (Producer) & Dulgan, J. (Director), Romero (1989). US: Paulist Pictures.

Kushner, J. (2012). Haitian farmers undermined by food aid. The Center for Public Integrity. https://www.publicintegrity.org/2012/01/11/7844/haitian-farmers-undermined-food-aid

Lumos (Report- 9-1-2017). Funding Haitian orphanages at the cost of children's rights Jamie Vernaede and Eugen Guilaume wearelumos.org https://www.wearelumos.org/resources/funding-haitian-orpahanges-cost-chidresn-rights/

Mauren, K. & Fitzgerald, J. (Executive Producers), & Miller, M. (Director). (2014) Poverty, Inc. US: Povertyinc.org.

New York Newsday, Wednesday, December 22, 1993. The Orphans, Home, Family and Country. By Molly Gordy.

Schwartz, R. (2013). Restaveks in Haiti. Unpublished manuscript.

Sprague, J. (2012). Paramilitarism and the assault on democracy in Haiti. Monthly Review Press: New York.

UNICEF (2016). UNICEF Annual Report 2015: Haiti. https://www.unicef.org/about/annual-report/files/Haiti_2015_COAR.pdf

Umoja, Akinyele (2011). Hating the root: Attacks on Vodou in Haiti. Blacks Agenda Report https://Blacksagendareport.com/content/hating-root-attacks-vodou-haiti

Walk Free Foundation (2016). The Global Slavery Index 2016. http//assest.globalslaveryindex.org/downloads/Global+Slavery+Index+2016pdf (accessed 1 November 2018)

Wochit News (March 20, 2017). Shots Fired at Former President of Haiti Aristide. youtube.com/watch?v=fmrshflxDmw

· 7 ·

GULU, UGANDA

"Why lock your window? If you don't want birds to fly in, monkeys to steal your
stuff or dogs to sleep on the bed, please lock your window when leaving the room."

ViaVia Resort, Entebbe, Uganda

Rebecca

*I didn't know much about Joseph Kony and the Lord's Resistance Army (LRA) until
I became the Country Director of Uganda in Gulu for the NGO—The Center for
Victims of Torture- CVT. Every Acholi person I meet has a story about the child
soldiers; from Ramsey the waiter, to my housekeeper, Irene—whose entire family
was taken, and one brother is missing and assumed with Kony, still. Most residents
of Gulu in northern Uganda and the surrounding villages have a connection; a family member abducted, raped, mutilated, or murdered. The traumatic history of this
period lives in Gulu.*

Joni

*Yes, somehow being here in Gulu with you this past month, I sense it too—in con-
versations, in passing comments, in the resiliency yet poverty of the people. When*

your friend and lawyer, Walter told us somewhat matter of factly, over an evening of wine, food and outdoor Congolese music—everything is outdoors here—that he had lost two men in his family to the conflicts, I thought trauma is normalized here. And when his ninety year old friend, WodOkello Lawoko, a survivor of Idi Amin's torture and the author of "The Dungeons of Nakasero" came to our table and showed us the scars and burns on the palm of his hand caused by Idi Amin's torture, Uganda's pain became a little more personal. The collective history of Uganda is trauma.

Rebecca

Yes, that's my work—addressing trauma. As of 2017, two years ago, the US and Ugandan military gave up the search for Kony in Uganda and, consequently made the way for me to become the country's director for Center for Victims of Torture. This NGO provides mental health and trauma counseling for victims of Joseph Kony's reign of terror in this region. Our organization receives two main sources of funding. The first source is from a trust fund supplied through the International Criminal Court (ICC) in the Hague, designated specifically for victims of Kony's Lord's Resistance Army (LRA) as part of the reparations. The other source is through the U.S. government earmarked for South Sudanese refugees fleeing to Uganda because of ongoing ethnic and tribal conflicts.

Gulu Terror

The terror and trauma in Gulu in the past several decades have subsided to some degree due to the movement of Joseph Rao Kony out of Uganda and into South Sudan, the Democratic Republic of the Congo and then into the Central African Republic where he is believed to be alive, but in ill health, with now only a small band of men remaining. Although he is no longer in Uganda, Joseph Kony became the face of the genocide and violence in Uganda for the past twenty-five or so years, in part because of media campaigns such as Kony 2012 and the Invisible Children, Inc. organization (Taylor, 2014). Kony became the embodiment of the violence, especially by western media; his atrocities were real. But the true history is more complicated and contradictory and, to be sure, he was not the only evil force at work. Nevertheless, Kony did perpetrate thousands of atrocities upon the Ugandan people of the North and left generational trauma, (the concept that trauma is passed along through our DNA), behind in Gulu especially among the Acholi people.

Joseph Kony is himself Acholi. He was born in 1961 and raised by poor farm working parents under a combination of Acholi nationalism and Christian fundamentalism. As a child Kony was a Catholic altar boy. Later he was drawn to a Holy Spirit Movement of the mid-80s in Uganda led by his charismatic cousin Alice Auma better known as Alice Lakwena. A spirit-medium who went insane, Lakwena took her name from a dead army officer who she was said to have channeled. Lakwena had a militant and idiosyncratic interpretation of the Old Testament viewing the government's National Resistance Movement (NRA) in southern Uganda to be of the devil (BBC, 2007; Reid, 2017).

Kony and the Lord's Resistance Army

Following the armed defeat of Lakwena and her militant followers in 1988 by Museveni's government forces, Kony formed the guerilla group, the Lord's Resistance Army (LRA). Kony said the LRA was fighting for the rights of the Acholi people who were marginalized in the turbulent politics of 1980s Uganda. Initially the LRA operated in northern Uganda and attempted to purify the Acholi people and turn Uganda into a theocracy. Under Kony's cult leadership, the LRA kidnapped boys to become child soldiers and young girls as sex slaves. The LRA terrorized the population through murder, abduction, mutilation, dismembering, and the burning of property. It is reported that hundreds of thousands have been its victims, with a large majority, children. Kony himself is said to have 60 wives and 42 children (Reid, 2017).

The LRA, under Kony, emerged after the fall of the Okello presidency in 1985–1986. Tito Okello, an Acholi, ousted Milton Obote who was also Acholi and then Okello himself was ousted by Yoweri Museveni, Uganda's then president. The LRA felt excluded from power after Obote and Okello both from the north were overthrown in a military rebellion and replaced by Museveni in 1886. Former soldiers from Okello's regime, including Acholi military officers fled north and were chased by Museveni's National Resistance Army (NRA). These government soldiers viewed the Acholi people as enemies of the state and proceeded to brutally kill, destroy property and sexually abuse and rape women in order to destroy the soul and fabric of the community (Reid, 2017). These atrocities certainly fueled the rage and anger of the Holy Spirit Movement and the LRA.

The Acholi people of northern Uganda were caught between the extremely violent Ugandan government army and the LRA who instilled fear in the community. Children were kidnapped regularly and trained as child soldiers. Attacks in the community included dismemberment of limbs, facial disfigurement and murder of community members. The newly named military unit under Museveni, the Uganda Peoples' Defense Force (UPDF) was either unwilling or unable to curtail the horrific ongoing violence directed at the Acholi people in the north of Uganda; it continued for nearly two decades from approximately 1994 through 2013 (Reid, 2017).

In 2014, the Obama administration sent troops to Uganda and in conjunction with the Ugandan military—an unlikely partner—went after the LRA. Although Kony himself was not captured, several of his leaders were captured and subsequently prosecuted by the ICC. In 2017 Ugandan and US troops gave up the search for Kony since he was driven out of northern Uganda and his army greatly diminished to about 100 soldiers.

Rebecca

One of Kony's extreme means of inflicting trauma in Gulu was by literally silencing the people. He put locks on their mouths to keep them from talking then threw away the keys. This was to warn people that this is what will happen to you if you talk. How did they eat? This was deep in the villages. When the NGO workers rescued them, they had to rip the locks from their mouths. The LRA also cut off hands, arms, feet and often ears.

Joni

Then I guess it is no wonder that you see so many security and police with guns—not guns, but big, long rifles. The people seem calm, gentle, so unbothered by a horrendous history—the history does not show in their outward demeanor. How do you survive and smile and carry on? For instance, your Acholi housekeeper and cook Irene's two brothers were taken as child soldiers at around eleven years of age. One of them escaped; he was badly beaten, and his legs broken. Her other brother is still with Kony. She speaks of all this calmly and with a smile on her face. She now has a son of nine years old and is a single mother. She is so beautiful, tall, ebony skin, slim; in the US or Europe she could be a model. She, as well as other Acholi, seem so calm, self-assured despite the trauma.

Rebecca

Yes, victims of Kony are everywhere. There are so many boda (motorcycle) drivers who like in Haiti, are one of the main means of transportation for the Ugandan people—a cheap but not always safe way of travel. I saw a woman whose skull was broken in a boda accident. Many of the drivers are young men who were former child soldiers. They were given motorcycles by NGO's once they were released or escaped from Kony, so they could make some sort of living. But you must be careful, because unexpectedly something can trigger the survivors' trauma and they can erupt. History lives here in the trauma and lives of the people but whether or not these people can or choose to memorialize these atrocities like Europe and the West does with the Holocaust or slavery, I am not sure.

And yes, they appear stable, but the situation is fragile now. The Ugandans are a fragile people, and the society is fragile. It can be toppled at any time. It is a superficial type of peace you are seeing. Museveni's current governmental regime suppresses the people too, just as past leaders have—maybe more subtle but yet present.

Museveni

Yoweri Kaguta Museveni is in his fifth term as president of Uganda and has revised the constitution and extended the presidential term limits so he can stay in power for life. He has been president since 1986 and was involved in rebellions that toppled Amin (1971–1979) and Milton Obote (1980–1985). Yoweri Kaguta Museveni claims to be an evangelical Christian and was given an honorary degree—Doctor of Law –the Humphrey School of Public Affairs, University of Minnesota in 1994 (Musinguzi, 2010).

Though Museveni is arguably less oppressive than his predecessors, nonetheless, he is a dictator. Museveni's military regime has been reported to torture and oppress any dissenting voices to his control. A recent example is Bobbi Wine, popular musician turned politician who speaks out against extended presidential term limits and a social media tax. Wine has been imprisoned for leading protests and speaking out (Soi, 2019). Like some other African nations' leaders, he seems to have little concern for the populace and issues such as a broken infrastructure—roads, bridges, electricity—as well rampant unemployment and poverty.

So, with Uganda's history of injustice and colonialization, it is somewhat surprising that in the area of incarceration, Uganda is somewhat progressive in its prison practices. It appears that prisons do take a rehabilitative approach, providing education, vocational training, recreation, mental health counseling, pre-release planning that supports prisoner's reengagement in society. The prisons do this while sorely understaffed and with an under-financed system (Jooly Gulu prison, personal communication, March 28, 2019; Musoke, 2016). There is no torture or solitary confinement and life sentences are very rare (Jooly Gulu prison, personal communication, March 28, 2019). Tragically most prisons are seriously overcrowded and slow to process sentencing for those waiting behind bars; however, in some ways, Uganda's prison system makes that of the US look almost medieval.

Uganda has been heralded for its approach to treating HIV and AIDS during the 1980s and 1990s, but there is still approximately 1.3 million Ugandans living with HIV with many unable to obtain the medicines they need. The punitive laws and stigmatizing attitudes towards sex, particularly homosexual practice, make the rise of HIV/AIDS under Museveni's regime probable. (Avert, 2019) HIV/AIDS, poverty, and poor health services have impacted life expectancy figures for decades; until recently the life expectancy was 47 years old. Although still low in 2016, the life expectancy increased to 59.8 years for men and 64.8 years for women (Wilson, 2018; World Health Organization, n.d.).

Uganda is precariously stable under Museveni as he appears to embrace dictatorship rather than democracy. Many Ugandans see this bent toward dictatorship as dangerous, and they are fearful. But Ugandans are also fearful to return to the horrors of the past. Many Ugandans think the current government situation is better than decades of violence and generations of trauma. 2021 will bring new presidential elections, and Museveni intends to win.

Then there is the task of remembering, memorializing, and uncovering truth about past atrocities and searching for accountability (De Yeaza & Fox, N., 2013). How committed is the current government to post-violence memory work in attempts to heal the nation, celebrate and mourn the past, and redress injustice? These are critical questions (De Yeaza and Fox, 2013; Ssenyonga, 2016). Remembering and memorializing is crucial for the healing of generational trauma and the notion that history will *not* repeat itself (Barsalou and Baxter, 2007). Young Ugandans need to know and remember their complicated history.

Joni

You and I talked about how in the West we memorialize tragedy: 911, the Holocaust, slavery, the civil rights movement, etc. And yes, we often have selective memory, and create history and memory from our own positionalities, but we do try to collectively remember our tragedies and triumphs through art, museums, memorial statues, days of mourning, specially designated holidays. I don't see much of that in Uganda. You said there are too many other pressing problems to care about collective memory. But I think collective memory in this case is paramount to going forward as a country and healing. Your work is all about remembering and uncovering the truth so people can move on. It may not be collective remembering but individual memory healing. Rebecca, and how are you in relation to this work in this country at this time? It is intense work, an intense location, an intense way to live. Does your work have meaning for you?

Rebecca

I was thinking about that today [long pause]; I have been thinking about that. [long pause] Now, it's just a job because I feel it is not so significant. I am not in direct services because of confidentiality. I can't meet with the clients face to face so it's hard to feel connected. I don't hear their stories. I am not in the counseling. I feel a little removed from the direct work though I know we are doing important work.

Despite having large administrative responsibilities, what brings me the greatest joy is helping to solve a problem. Since I am a hands-on person, I do enjoy working with the staff. During weekly staff meetings, I usually have some sort of ice breaker to build community—you know, I learned a lot of that from you. I watched you when you did community work in Brooklyn and how you had group activities, I learned from you.

Joni

That makes me very happy. I am so proud of you and even though you do not do direct service your work is highly significant though it is primarily administrative. You have been promoted to Senior Level Management in the field and so young; you have paid your dues—in Haiti, Jordan, the Congo, and now Uganda. I do not see your work as a drop in the bucket, either. Your organization, under your oversight and direction, heals individuals one at a time; individuals are moving away from trauma, getting well from the trauma inflicted by the LRA.

Once again, I return to the question of faith. How do you reconcile your faith, keep your faith amid abuse of faith and Christ; in the face of cults and religious tourism? By religious tourism I mean mostly Americans going down to a poor country on "mission's trips" for the purpose of evangelism and/or short-term help—medical, construction, etc. But basically, it seems to me the Americans or individuals from more affluent countries around the world end up having some sort of "cultural experience." It's not all bad but it sometimes seems patronizing and voyeuristic. What's your experience? And what is the church in Uganda doing in terms of responding to the trauma?

Rebecca

Well, Joseph Kony and his cousin Alice's movement was just plain demonic in nature and a Satanic thing. Kony often said he was Jesus Christ. But my faith continues strong despite these twisted "spiritual" people. There are some Christians doing trauma work like Samaritan's Purse and World Vision who are doing work in mental health; they have a different approach than we have. There is another organization, Tuta Pona providing mental health services who I think are out of Milwaukee.

I don't see so much religious tourism in Uganda—it is too far from the US; not like I did in Haiti. The people here are really missionaries. Sometimes not very wise, but they are really missionaries. They live in remote areas and are sincere to a calling. They actually make a sacrifice, and it's not religious tourism. Some of them I saw in the Congo, Beni- a very dangerous area. There were these two White women, a Dutch and a Canadian, who are now in their middle 50s. They have been in the Congo since the 1980s and have given their lives to the work. Both married Congolese man. One said that if it were not for the church praying—getting on their knees and praying, they would not have made it. Also, a White couple who were in Uganda in the 1980s when the byword for Uganda was craziness "paid their dues." God called them and they risked and sacrificed their lives. That is all good and that is not religious tourism. They were here during the LRA insurgency.

Most of the survivors of the Amin era are dead since the population is young here and the average life expectancy is somewhere in the mid-40s, I think. I met a woman who I thought I might rent a house from; she was in her 70s and said her husband was brutally murdered by Amin. So that memory is still here—Amin, the self-proclaimed King of the Nile.

Aminism

"There is freedom of speech, but I cannot guarantee freedom after speech"—the words of Idi Amin which certainly proved true. Anyone who spoke out, or was even perceived to speak out against him, was tortured and executed. He also believed that death and sacrifice of a country's people was necessary for a leader to achieve law and order.

And many thousands did die for his so-called law and order; their mass graves in many cases have yet to be uncovered and the bodies removed (Lawoko, 2005); the International Court of Justice which never tried Amin estimated 300,000 Ugandans died during his regime but human rights organizations estimate half a million (Wall, 2016).

Idi Amin Dada Oumee was a Ugandan politician and military officer who was the President of Uganda from 1971 to 1979. His rule was notorious for its brutality and oppressiveness. Amin was born either in Koboko or Kampala to a Kakwa father and Lugbara mother. In 1946 he joined the King's African Rifles (KAR) of the British Colonial Army. Initially a cook, he rose to the position of lieutenant, taking part in British actions against Somali rebels in the Shifta War and then the Mau rebels in Kenya. Following Uganda's independence from the United Kingdom in 1962, Amin remained in the armed forces, rising to the position of major and being appointed Commander of the Army in 1965. Aware that Ugandan President Milton Obote was planning to arrest him for misappropriating army funds, Amin launched a 1971 military coup and declared himself President (Lawoko, 2005).

During his years in power, Amin shifted from being a pro-western ruler enjoying considerable Israeli support to being backed by Libya's Muammar Gaddafi, Zaire's Mobutu Sese Seko, Brezhnev's Soviet Union, and Honecker's East Germany. In 1975, Amin became the chairman of the Organization of African Unity (OAU), a Pan-Africanist group designed to promote solidarity among African states. During the 1977–1979 period, Uganda was a member of the UN Commission on Human Rights. In 1977, when the UK broke diplomatic relations with Uganda, Amin declared he had defeated the British and added "CBE", for "Conqueror of the British Empire", to his title. Radio Uganda then announced his entire title: "His Excellency President for Life, Field Marshal Alhaji Dr. Idi Amin Dada, VC, DSO, MC, CBE."

As Amin's rule progressed into the late 1970s, growing dissent against his persecution of certain ethnic groups and political dissidents, along with Uganda's very poor international standing in the world led to Tanzanian soldiers to capture Kampala, Uganda's capital. This forced Amin and colleagues into exile first in Libya then in Saudi Arabia where he died in 2003 (Reid, 2017).

Westerners often remember Amin from the seven days in Entebbe (1976) where an Air France jet with 239 passengers was held hostage by Ugandan armed soldiers to focus on the plight of Palestinians. Israeli soldiers eventually invaded the Entebbe airport to release the hostages but not before

Amin strutted his persona across the international stage. But most of all, his infamous 8-year reign is remembered for his torture and brutal killing of his supposed enemies or anyone who voiced dissent and the culture of terror he perpetrated (Laweko, 2005).

Joni

Meeting an actual victim of Amin's regime, WodOkello Lawoko, who was the Head of Programmes in Radio Uganda at the time Idi Amin took power, however briefly, sticks in my memory. I remember his scarred hand, and now I read his book where he lays out the torture and pain of the Amin era in such personal and graphic detail. He witnessed friends and family disappearing, witnessed torture, and was tortured and imprisoned himself. You can almost feel how he wants to leave memories behind so that it will never happen again; a brave soul, in my mind.

But from my limited reading of Ugandan history, I understand that even before Amin and the British colonialization, this region that is now called Uganda had experienced slave and sex trade and labor, and violence for centuries. There is this struggle between the tribe and pre-colonial identity and the nation-state. People for the most part belong to their tribe first then to the nation—Uganda (Reid, 2017 p. 285). So, throughout Kony, Amin and the British colonialization, it has known violence, but cooperation as well for centuries. How do the people function so seemingly well, as I see them carry on—calm and gentle, maybe docile, as you say?

Rebecca

Again, the Ugandans are a fragile people. If they protest, they will be shot. They have no voice; they cannot speak. There is fear and suppression. The price of peace under this current regime is docility as someone told me, "we are a broken people; there is fear in us; and there is no fight in us anymore." Despite this, I think what you are also seeing is resiliency. I see it everywhere, not only in Uganda. I see it in the Congo, Haiti, Kenya, America—the Black race has resiliency. God has given them the gift of resiliency. I don't know how they have the strength to get up in the morning, to keep going. No jobs, high taxes, no hope. Africa has made me tired.

Joni

How so? How do you mean?

Rebecca

My people. My race. I mean emotionally and spiritually tired. I just wonder what is going to happen to the Black race. There are real problems with Blacks across the board. There are seriously so many deep spiritual problems with us as a race—intrinsically and extrinsically. We have problems as a race. We don't promote our own culture and the riches of it—we westernize too much. And we don't help each other as we should. I want to break this debilitating mindset. I just wish I knew what could be done; the answer to help us. On the one hand, I feel very good in Africa. I want to help the Black race; how to get us together mentally, spiritually and emotionally. Yes, I'm tired but I love Africa—the people, the race, the continent.

Figure 7.1   Rebecca and Joni writing in Uganda

Joni

Yes, so overwhelming, yet beautiful, warm and frightening in so many ways—that is my experience thus far in my travels to Africa. I think about riding on a Kenya Airways flight (the pride of Africa) to Nairobi from JFK with a transfer in Entebbe. The middle-aged Ugandan gentleman sitting next to me gazed over at the book I was reading, A History of Modern Uganda, and pointed to the word "modern" and chuckled lightly and said, "let's see if you find it so."

A Young Uganda

Uganda's population is one of the world's youngest. About 78% of Ugandans are under 30 years old, with the median age at 15 years old, second only to Niger (Myers, 2016; UNESCO).

In addition, Uganda has one of the highest birth rates in the world which along with poverty makes it susceptible to corruption and the exploitation of children. According to the US Department of State, Uganda is a Tier 2 country which means it does not fully meet the minimum standards for the elimination of human, in particular, child trafficking but is making efforts to do so (US State Department, 2019).

In other words, human and child trafficking, forced labor and sexual exploitation is present, and adoption is enmeshed in this process. More than 1600 Ugandan children have been adopted since 1999 (Aljazeera, 2018). It is uncertain how many of these adoptions represented true orphans and how many are criminal child trafficking cases. In Uganda a market for adoptions has been created through organizations like the European Adoption Consultants and God's Mercy Orphanage. Both are being investigated by the FBI for deceiving Ugandan birth parents into believing that their children are being taken to the US for an education and will be returned;—and deceiving American adoptive parents that the children are truly orphans. It is all about money, (Kaye, n.d.) and not unique to Uganda. In almost all these cases whether legitimate or fraudulent the adoptive parents are White, and the child is Black African.

Joni

This is not an unfamiliar story. We saw it in Haiti. In terms of the two of us, can we sort through and center on legitimate adoptions where the children were really orphans like you were? What do you think about the statement that I have often heard, "A loving family should matter more than the color of the parents when considering adoption." In other words, love trumps color or race.

Rebecca

I haven't heard that phrase. But I don't know if that is true necessarily now that I am older; now that I can see race, systemic and institutional racism mainly in the US. I've been to other predominantly White countries and it is different—the UK, Netherlands, Czech Republic, France, etc. Slavery was not endemic to these countries as it was in the US. They colonized people, yes, there was apartheid as in South Africa, yes; but slavery was on the soil of the US. In the US it is slavery, Jim Crow, KKK, Civil Rights, mass incarceration, and police brutality, generational racism and discrimination.

Don't get me wrong. There is a glass ceiling in Europe for immigrants but then again it is a totally different system of government—social welfare but everyone is more equal instead of a free market system and capitalism. There is more equality in Europe and Canada from what I can see. So, I think for a White American family adopting a Black child, especially how the US is structured, it is difficult. If the White parents don't understand and become allies against racism and advocates for civil rights, it is bad for the Black child.

A Black child is cute when they are a baby. But they grow up to be a big man— 18, 19, 21 years old. It's cute to carry around a little Black baby- it's a celebrity trend—adopting Black babies—Madonna, and others. They seem to adopt mostly Black boys. Yes, they will have privilege because they are with privileged parents, but this will be difficult for the boys.

Joni

Would Black parents be better? I guess I ask because I struggled with this for a time when we first adopted you. I told you about the Black couple who came forward to adopt you once your Dad and I had made our intentions known that we wanted you. This couple from New Jersey evidently had already adopted a couple of babies from the orphanage and for some time they had your birth certificate in their possession with intentions of adopting you. But they were very slow in moving on it. So, the orphanage assumed that you were available, and the Black couple weren't going to go through with the adoption. We then met you in Haiti and decided we wanted you and moved ahead with the adoption process. As part *of that process, we needed your original birth certificate, but this couple had it in their possession.*

So, one evening in the summer of 1990, they brought your birth certificate to the Brooklyn Tabernacle Church and said they still wanted to adopt you. So now Mom Workman and other heads of the orphanage had two couples who wanted you—one White and one Black. I remember sitting in an office, your Dad had been praying feverishly, and I was crying. I foolishly said two things: one, I said, "maybe she would be better with a Black family" and two "maybe we should ask Rebecca who she wants to be her mommy and daddy." To which Mom Workman responded, it doesn't matter what color you are and Rebecca's a child, we can't put that on her. We are the adults, and God will have to make this decision. And God did.

Rebecca

Hmm …. Black parents aren't always the best choice because I know some Black parents are not good parents, either. The statement you said is very complicated. Naturally, if it was a choice between having no parents and having White parents—White parents are a better choice.

Sleeping in the Same Bed

Joni

Well, you have me and I have you. Now almost thirty years later, we still sleep in the same bed sometimes. In this disturbing age of hyper sexuality, the phrase "sleeping in the same bed" may have certain connotations for some—but in our context it is all innocence, comfort and nurturing.

You were nine years old, almost ten, and a skinny little thing. When I arrived at the orphanage, you latched onto me physically, sliding up next to me between the crowd of people, looking up at me with those big longing eyes. For the next week you wouldn't let me go.

That entire week I was in Carrefour, you held onto my arm as if saying don't go anywhere without me—don't you dare leave me behind, I am part of you now. But especially at night, you wanted to sleep with me in the guest quarters. I remember it being very hot and I was all sweaty, but you nestled up to me with your arms around me; you wanted to be cuddled like a baby. I had no choice but to spend my nights sweating profusely because you needed the warmth and the nurturing, and I needed to bond with you. I didn't mind really; I loved you already—I wanted to be close, to bond, to nurture. But because it was so hot, I lay awake with you in my arms falling in and out of sleep trying to catch what breeze I could from the screened windows, listening to the sounds of the Haitian nights, far away music, voices, night birds and the early morning roosters crowing. You didn't seem to mind the heat and slept soundly in my arms. So now nearly 30 years later, I sleep in the same bed with you in Gulu under very different circumstances—but still hot.

Rebecca

I remember saying, "Can you speak!?" After you abruptly stormed into my bedroom at about 4 or 5 am while it was still dark and woke me up. You were clearly upset almost hysterical but couldn't seem to talk. Then you managed to say, "There is something in my bed!"

Joni

At first, I couldn't talk or scream. I was frozen. I was petrified. I could hardly get any words out of my mouth; I was so frightened. My recollection is that you said "What is wrong? What is wrong, Mom?"

You gave me my own beautifully decorated bedroom with an attached bath, which I loved, in your large eight room gated home in what is called the Malibu of Gulu. But it is still the bush. I had been warned to make sure the windows were closed tightly with the screen so that no creatures could enter, but I had suffered a mild heat stroke the previous day—too much sun, the pool, and dehydration—and wanted the cool breeze of the Ugandan evening to come through my window. So, I kept the window open.

As time goes by, I have been questioned and stick to my story. I awoke about 5:45 am and it was still dark outside. It was the rainy season in Uganda. I got up to go to the bathroom and to unplug my cell phone and plug yours in—as I had promised I would do before going to bed. Then I took my phone back to the big double bed and looked at a few text messages. I was fully awake. I laid the phone down on the foot of the bed and then I lay back down. A few moments later, I heard a rustling sound and at first thought it was the guard outside on the property making his rounds, but then I turned my head to the other side of the bed and there as God is my witness, I saw a foot long Black creature who seemed to be slithering across the bed—I did not take time to observe closely what it was but flung myself from the bed, lunged out of the room, and ran pounding on your bedroom door.

Rebecca

I went into the bedroom and picked up my new kitten (who I had gotten to catch mice) and threw him on the bed. You yelled, "It is going to get killed; there is something in there! What if it is a snake!" Then I thought, oh man, maybe you are right—if it is a snake, it could wrap itself around the cat. The cat ran out quickly anyway; it did not want to stay near the bed.

Joni

Then I remember you slamming the bedroom door. And saying, "This is why the cat is here! The cat is here for this purpose!" I thought it could have been one of three creatures: a large lizard, a rat, or a snake.

Rebecca

For it to be a rat or snake or a possum, it would have to get through the bars in the window. It certainly came from outside. Where else could it come from? You said maybe from behind the toilet but that's too small, come on, you are describing something bigger. This is the bush they are coming inside even though everything is clean. Creatures are attracted to food so whatever it was probably looking for the cat and dog food. The three animals you described are nocturnal; their activity is mostly done at night.

Joni

Then you started blaming me and fussing, "It's your fault. I have lived here for four months and I haven't had any creatures like this—maybe you were dreaming or saw a shadow. You are causing me stress. S -T-R-E-S-S, you spelled it out, and I don't need stress. From now on you close those windows; I'll buy you a fan."

I know it was my fault for leaving the window open, but you didn't have to blame me when I was traumatized. I insisted upon sleeping with you in your bed. You protested but I would sleep with you for the rest of my time in Gulu.

Rebecca

Yes, you insisted upon sleeping in my bed until the morning when the housekeeper and gardener could check out the bedroom. We went to sleep beat, hot, stressed and traumatized. The next morning when the housekeeper, Irene, came, she too was unwilling to go into the bedroom in case it was a poisonous snake or something dangerous. Once the gardener came, they went in and thoroughly searched. The mattress was upended, every nook and cranny cleaned and explored. We concluded that the creature, whatever it was, was long gone out the window. But this creature would be the topic of conversation for days to come. I kept thinking there is cleaning every day, what was the creature trying to find? And what I found a little weird, it was on the bed next to the wall; that's what I find odd. And you shouldn't have left the window open—this is Africa, after all.

Joni

I know it is my fault. Where else could it come from? The only way they can come is from outside. I remember we kept rehashing what happened that night, and how the creature moved slowly when I jumped from the bed, and how at first, I couldn't talk. But I didn't scream, either. I am not a screamer. No, I am not a screamer. Even when I was giving birth to Nathan and Matthew in the hospital delivery room, when plenty of other women were screaming, I didn't. Then you said, "That's why I am having a C-section!"

Rebecca

A snake moves slowly. What was it size-wise? The width? I was trying to think if it were rat or possum it had to be small enough to go through the window bars. I started online research and concluded that it was probably attracted to food but there was no food in the bedroom, and we cleaned every day.

Joni

Toward the end of my month in Uganda, we finally figured out what the mysterious house guest was after talking with several native Ugandan's of Acholi descent, one a lawyer and the other a diplomat who works for Nobel Prize organizations in Scandinavia; both grew up in northern Uganda and Gulu in particular. When describing the night of the creature's visit and the creature itself, right away they responded. "Oh, that was an Obaa." There is no exact English translation for Obaa because Obaas do not live in North America. A rough translation, however, is a Gambian Pouched Rat. In Acholi regions they are known as the "thief" because they go into homes looking to steal metal objects like knives and forks with which they sharpen their teeth, then bury the objects. They are harmless to humans and have been known to be kept as pets outside Africa. In Africa, in some places they are a valued source of bush meat and eaten on a stick. There was some relief now that I know what was in my bed, but I still insisted upon sleeping with you the rest of the trip.

Rebecca

At first, I said, "No you are not sleeping with me; you better not snore." But how could I say no, my mom now needed my protection, warmth and security.

Joni

This time we are in Gulu, Uganda and she is a grown professional woman with a career, a home, goals, accomplishments. I am staying in her home doing research for this book and writing. This time I am sleeping in her bed, and she is taking care of my fears.

References

Aljazeera, (2018, October 10). *Adoption Inc: The baby business: How demand from US families seeking to adopt babies from abroad has paved the way for exploitation and fraud.*

Avert, (2019). Global information and education on HIV and AIDS. https: www.avert.org/ professionals/hiv-around-world/sub-saharan-africa/uganda. Accessed: February 19, 2019.

Barsalou, J. & Baxter, V. (2007). The urge to remember: The role of memorials in social reconstruction and transitional justice. USIP Stabilization and Reconstruction Series, 5.

BBC News, (2007, January 18). Uganda's mystic rebel leader dies. http:// news.bbc.co.uk/2/hi/ africa/6274313.stm. Accessed: February 19, 2019.

De Yeaza, C. & Fox, N. (2013). Narratives of mass violence: The role of memory and memorialization in addressing human rights violations in post-conflict Rwanda and Uganda. *Societies without borders.* 8:3.

Kaye, R. (n.d). Kids for sale, part 1 and 2, CNN—An exclusive investigation. https//www.cnn. cp,/specials/kids-for-sale. Accessed: February 19, 2019.

Lawoko, W. (2005). The Dungeons of Nakasero: A true story and painful experience. Stockholm: Forfattares Bokmaskin.

Musinguzi, J. (2010, January 17). Makerere graduation special: Museveni, Kawawa get honorary degrees. *The Observer.*

Musoke, R. (2019, April 15). How Uganda built best prison service in Africa. Retrieved from https://www.independent.co.ug/author/mronald/

Myers, J. (2016). The world's 10 youngest populations are all in Africa. World Economic Forum. https://www.weforum.org/agenda/2016/05/the-world-s-10-youngest-countries-are-all-in-africa/

Reid, R. J. (2017). The history of modern Uganda. Cambridge: Cambridge University Press.

Soi, C. (2019, May 4). Uganda: Bobi Wine vows to keep fighting despite recent arrest. Al Jazeera.

Ssenyonga, F.N. (2016). The emerging role of community museums in Uganda: The need for capacity building among managers. Museum International. No. 269–270.

Taylor, A. (2014, December 16). Was #Kony2012 a failure? The Washington Post. https://www.washingtonpost.com/news/worldviews/wp/2014/12/16/was-kony2012-a-failure/?utm_term=.75310286a8b3

US State Department (n.d). Uganda 2018 trafficking in persons report. Retrieved May 11, 2019. https://www.state.gov/j/tip/rls/tiprpt/countries/2018/282772.htm

UNESCO (n.d). Total population by age group- Uganda, 2017. Retrieved May 10, 2019: http://uis.unesco.org/en/country/ug?theme=culture

Wall, K. (2016, December 27) Ghost Stories: Idi Amin's torture chambers. Harper's: International Women's Media Foundation. http://www.iwmf.org/reporting/ghost-stories-idi-amins-torture-chambers/

Wilson, Y. (2018, November 8) The Borgen Project. Life expectancy in Uganda. https://borgenproject.org/life-expectancy-in-uganda/

World Health Organization (n.d.). Uganda releases preliminary results of the 2016 Uganda population HIV impact assessment. Retrieved May 10, 2019 https://www.afro.who.int/news/uganda-releases-preliminary-results-2016-uganda-populatuon-hiv-impact-assessment

US State Department (n.d). Uganda 2018 trafficking in persons report. Retrieved May 11, 2019. https://www.state.gov/j/tip/rls/tiprpt/countries/2018/282772.htm

UNESCO (n.d). Total population by age group- Uganda, 2017. Retrieved May 10, 2019. http://uis.unesco.org/en/country/ug?theme=culture

· 8 ·

BUNIA, THE DEMOCRATIC REPUBLIC OF THE CONGO

"The conquest of the earth, which mostly means the taking it away from those who have a different complexion or slightly flatter noses than ourselves, is not a pretty thing when you look into it too much."

Joseph Conrad

Rebecca

I left Bunia, the second largest city in eastern Congo the Democratice Republic of Congo, (DRC), two months before another outbreak of Ebola. I was an expat but also considered a Muzungu by all the Congolese even though I am a Black American. Muzungu comes from the Swahili and Bantu language of the Eastern and Great Lakes region of Africa. Muzungu generally means White man but it does apply to White women and foreigners, too. So, I am a Muzungu, a foreigner.

Joni

I read that Muzungu literally means "someone who roams around" or "wanderer" coming from zunga and kizunguzungu meaning dizziness. (Chemi Che-Mponda, 2019) I think you fit that description well. You roam around the world with dizzying ease; so proud of you in that regard.

Rebecca

When a friend described you to me, she said "Your Mom is a free spirit." Perhaps there is a little of the Muzungu in you as well. I love you to the moon and back.

Joni

Mmmm—going to the Congo is kind of like going to the moon and back. I never got there—the closest I came was Western Uganda near the border when you worked in DRC. This was 2017 when over a dozen UN peacekeepers were murdered and many more injured in the region of Beni. I planned to visit you and was preparing my paperwork when the US State Department advised no travel to the Congo. I met you in Uganda instead. On the return trip, my plane was turned around over the Atlantic because of fierce storms in New York so I spent three days in Brussels. While there, I remember looking for traces of Belgium's history of its brutal colonization of the Congo. I found little. I learned later that the African museum was closed for five years for renovations.

The Silence of History

The Belgium Africa Museum located in Brussels is one of the world's largest collections of African art acquired through the years of DRC's colonization. The newly opened museum is not without controversy as the former Congolese President, Joseph Kabila, and the DRC government want many of the artifacts returned to the Congo. The racist and cruel Belgian regime does not own or deserve to have the artwork that belongs to the people of DRC whose history has been too long silenced (Boffey, 2018).

DRC is comparable to other African nations: politically unstable, wrought with natural and man-made disasters, corrupted, and pervasive poverty. In addition, the Congo has experienced protracted conflict resulting in the deaths of more than five million people and most recently an Ebola epidemic the World Health Organization (WHO) has declared an international health emergency. The Congo is the second largest country in Africa, about the same size as Western Europe. It is by far one of the richest countries in the world in natural resources, blessed with every type of mineral including deposits of gold, copper, uranium, coltan, diamonds, cobalt, and oil. Yet the Congo is consistently rated lowest in the Human Development Index with a considerable large part of its population suffering from poor health and nutrition, high mortality rates, low levels of education, poor infrastructure, starvation and disease (Food Agriculture Organization, 2018).

According to John Snow in his 2013 BBC article, *DR Congo: Cursed by its natural wealth*, "the Congo's apocalyptic present is a direct product of decisions and actions taken over the past five centuries." In the late 15th Century, the Congo like many African countries was socially sophisticated with an aristocracy and an impressive civil service. The inhabitants of the Congo lived in tribes or kingdoms, and they had territories with boundaries that they defended. There were walled cities with armies, complex trade relationships, long distance trade routes, alliances, and enemies. Indeed, in some places there was even a 2000-year history of contact with the outside world; the people of the Congo were neither primitives, cannibals nor savages. There is clear evidence that these people had contact with the Egyptians, and that their music was all the rage in the Pharaoh's court (Ahmad & Awan, 2017).

Portuguese traders arrived in the 1480s. They realized they had stumbled upon a land of vast natural wealth, rich in resources—especially human flesh, as Congo was the home to an abundant supply of strong, disease-resistant Africans. As with many colonial powers, the Portuguese soon realized this supply of flesh would be easier to exploit if the country was in a chaotic state (Snow, 2013). The Portuguese supported and armed rebel groups within the Congo and did their best to destroy any indigenous political force by sewing chaos and terror by undermining Congolese armies, murdering kings, slaughtering elites and leaders. Mutiny, strife and conflict was encouraged. By the 1600s, the once-mighty and sophisticated kingdom had disintegrated into a leaderless, chaotic mini-state locked in perpetual civil war. Slaves who were the by product victims of fighting were carried to the Western coast and shipped to the Americas (Snow, 2013).

"This first engagement with Europe formed the bedrock for the rest of Congo's history and was structurally embedded in the social, political and cultural fabric as evidenced in the Congo one sees today. To further understand its impact, close scrutiny of the phenomenon of colonialism is necessary to appreciate the degree to which it influenced not only the economic and political development of the Congo, but also the peoples' perceptions of themselves" (Khapoya, 1994, p. 99). In the late 19th Century, between 1884–1885, the Berlin West Africa Conference began what is commonly referred to as the "Scramble for Africa" effectively divided up the African continent. In attendance were the colonial powers of Great Britain, France, Spain, Portugal,

Germany, and Belgium. The Conference created artificial state boundaries as well as a colonial system that was in effect for the next sixty years.

Out of all the African countries colonized by the Europeans, the Congo's relationship with Belgium is distinct. Numerous accounts mark it as two decades of the cruelest rule ever inflicted on a colonized people. This relationship would continue a half-century later after the country's independence in the 1960s by the Belgium's violent intervention in Congolese politics (Hochschild, 1998).

The distinction begins with the Congo as the only country to be the personal property of a European king. In 1885, a year after the Berlin conference, King Leopold II established the Congo Free State, which was not a Belgian colony, but a personal possession owned by him. The Congo made King Leopold the largest landowner on the planet and the most notorious. The king of tiny Belgium, Leopold II, made claim to the Congo with a land mass nearly ninety times the size of his own kingdom (Khapoya, 1994). His mission was to "civilize" the Africans, but he was really interested in securing the rich raw materials from the colony for his country. For over 23 years, he made the Congo into his personal fiefdom. He reaped an enormous fortune in ivory and turned the Congolese into slave laborers to gather wild rubber. In his book *Heart of Darkness*, Joseph Conrad wrote about this economic exploitation by King Leopold and control of the Congolese people highlighting the mistreatment of the women, the destruction of the culture, language and the physical and psychological destruction of human beings. Under this King's reign, it is estimated that about 10 million Congolese died due to disease and starvation (Hochshild, 1998).

This colonial period impacted the social, political, cultural and economic conditions of the Congolese. In addition to these impacts, there was profound psychological impact, especially around the issue of race. Imperialism carries with it attitudes of racial superiority that justified exploitation and created paradigms of racial inferiority in the colonized (Smith, 1982). This impact remains; and both the colonizer and the colonized carry colonialism in their minds long after the state has gained independence (Ngugi wa Thiong'o, 1986).

This concept is evidenced in one aspect by the bleaching phenomena pervasive in today's Congolese society as well as in Nigeria, Sierra Leone, parts of Asia, the Caribbean and the Middle East. Even in the United States, it is present and a global multi-billion-dollar industry preying on women and sometimes men who go to great lengths to have lighter skin. And, surprisingly skin-bleaching is on the rise rather than diminishing among educated urban women in the Global South, low- and middle-income countries in Asia, Africa, Latin America and the Caribbean (Del Guidance and Yves, 2002; Ntshingla, 2005).

Rebecca

In the Congo I was first exposed to this on a field mission when we stopped at a local supermarket and a Sierra Leonean colleague, Rosie, stopped to buy toiletries which included some bleaching creams. I was not aware that this was what she bought until she pointed out that she wanted to have brownish skin, sun-kissed skin, and the cocoa butter in the lotion was going to help her. However, this is so far from the truth. Not only do these creams ruin ones' skin, but they contain very harsh chemicals like mercury which is toxic to the bloodstream. These women, and sometimes men, are so addicted to attaining lighter skin that they are not concerned about the side effects which cause serious harm to one's health. Lighter skin is considered a status symbol and a sign that one is of a higher class. Light skin in the Congo provides status, higher paying jobs, and more romantic prospects because the women are considered more beautiful. Many women go to great lengths to secure these items, even if it means not having enough money for food and running the risk of potential criminal penalties because some products are illegal.

Joni

This is deep and painful stuff. Yes, this decolonizing of the mind is necessary for both Whites and Blacks. This decolonization is an active moving away from ideas that hold people in subjugation and exploitation of one another in their thinking; I think it takes deep reflection, confessions and a breaking from denial. It goes back to the sunbathing and appropriation we talked about. I think it ties into assimilationist thinking. So, you may not have segregationist thinking (one group of people is inferior to another group of people), but you may have assimilationist thinking that there is a certain White standard that individuals need to aspire to whether conscious or unconscious. This is still racist. Ibram Kendi talks about these three mental frameworks of race: segregationist, assimilationist and anti-racist (Kendi, 2015). I keep trying to decolonize my own mind.

Rebecca

Another experience of race I recall was when I was an area manager with Medair in Beni while managing a field team including both expatriate and national Congolese staff. My direct reports were the managerial expatriates, and their direct reports were the national staff. The Sierra Leonean colleague, Rosie, I spoke about was a direct report to me. She was a health manager in an emergency health program funded by USAID. As an African expat, she was consistently undermined by her staff and expatriates for being perceived as inexperienced or incapable.

Although she was not experienced in project management, she was committed and hard- working and relied heavily on my assistance to learn her role, especially finance budgeting and logistics. She was learning and developing. A second challenge was she didn't speak French well, and when she did it was with a heavy West African accent. Due to the challenges of recruiting French speaking expatriate staff, we had an internship program providing French speakers valuable field experience fitting them for potential roles as managers leading emergency health and water, sanitation, and hygiene (WASH) programs.

During my tenure we recruited a young male intern, Claude, who was a French nurse. Claude was very eager to embark on a managerial role in the Congo. He was assigned to work with Rosie because her location in Beni was one of the most challenging with twenty-one health facilities in rebel held territories.

I think this French young man believed that he could do a better job than Rosie, and I believe race played a factor. I have many documented examples of him undermining her and turning her staff against her. But one incident sticks in my mind. One day while on Rest & Relaxation (RNR) in Gisenyi, Rwanda, I got an early morning phone call from a hysterically crying Rosie. It seems staff members wrote anonymous feedback in the office suggestion box. Rosie and another staff opened the box and read the notes which were mostly about Rosie.

The comments were scathing, personal, and subjective. One comment was about how she dressed and was always naked! Another attacked her skills and how unfit she was for the job. Another suggested that she be replaced by the intern because he was more qualified and could speak better French! She told me this by phone, and I assured her that I would address the comments upon return to work. I was not in the mind frame to think as I was supposed to be unwinding and decompressing from the work.

However, I did spend some time thinking about the comments, and the meaning behind them. I felt the comments were sexist. Rosie was the only female manager on that team; and to me, there was also an underlying racial dynamic. The comments attacked her skills, her ability to manage and lead a team. They attacked her knowledge, as one even questioned how she got the job. Also, they specifically requested for the young male intern to manage them because he "had more knowledge than her" and "could lead them better" without really knowing his background and experience and why he was hired as an intern and not as a manager.

When I went back to Beni, I addressed her whole team and asked them why they felt this young man was more fit than their manager who went through a fair and transparent recruitment process and was selected for the job because she was the best suited for it. They did not know Claude, the intern, as he had been working with them for only a few months. They had been working with Rosie for close to a year. My conclusion, he was male and White.

I had heard about character assassinations before and how pervasive it was in the Black community. So, when I saw it being played out in Africa, I was deeply saddened. It hurt to see how Black African people were seemingly so quick to blindly accept the authority and superiority of another person due to the color of their skin. It became apparent that they did not know this intern's background, his qualifications, and why he was placed as an intern instead of a program manager in Beni. My conclusion was that whether consciously or subconsciously they based their feelings on the color of his skin. White skin, especially male, said to them "he knows more than the Black female colleague and was more qualified and experienced than she was as a result he should replace her."

I confronted this mindset, and I am sure it was not altogether conscious but a product of colonial programming. When I asked my staff why they believed Claude was more experienced and more suited to be their boss, I was not really expecting an answer but was challenging a way of thinking. I wanted them to become aware of their own implicit biases which reflected how they saw themselves in the backdrop of racial inferiority and White supremacy. As I saw it, this thinking kept them subservient, dependent, and ignorant. Their answers were not forthcoming. So, I answered my own question. The staff became visibly uncomfortable. You see, Africans are not very happy with their colonial past and their colonial masters who kept them bound for centuries; however, they are sometimes not aware that they continue to practice colonialism upon their own people and esteem their White masters in visible ways like bleaching their skin or undermining one another.

Joni

I get this—the oppressed coming back and being the oppressor or at least practicing oppression. I guess I have two qualifying statements in response to what you have said. First, I think that we need to be careful about characterizing all Africans or Blacks, or many Africans, into categories or patterns of behavior—character

assassinators, unaware or ignorant because I am sure that is true for some individu-
als but grouping people that way I think is racist.

Also, I would add that Whites' mindset has to change too. When we continue
to make racism only Black peoples' issue—that is a problem. It is all our burden, all
our responsibility, all our issues. How we decolonize our minds as we decolonize our
policies, as we decolonize our behavior seems to me the work of all of us.

You know as we continue to unpack race, I think about race as a relatively
modern concept—developed during the Enlightenment. And I think about how all
humans originated in Africa. You were explaining that to me the other day. We are
99.9% the same.

99.9% the Same

Launched in 1990 and completed in 2003, the Human Genome Project was
the world's largest international collaborative biological project. It was funded
by the National Institutes for Health and other private and public groups
around the world, tapping the expertise of the world's best scientists. In sim-
ple terms, the project was designed to sequence the DNA in human cells.
The analysis of the data is still in relatively initial stages, but advances from
the project are already seen in medicine and biotechnology including genetic
testing for predisposition to cancer, Alzheimer's, and liver diseases. There are
also ramifications for criminal justice, adoption and paternity queries in addition to the immense impact in the medical sciences.

But the project and its findings also extended to the defining of "race."
Craig Venter, one of the chief private scientists in the project, stated early
on that "race is not a scientifically valid construct" (McCann-Mortimer,
Augoustinos and LeCouteur, 2004). The findings also state that we as
human beings are 99.9% the same as it relates to DNA (National Human
Genome Research Institute, 2019). This research and many other archeo-
logical and genetic studies have ascertained that Homo sapiens originated
in Africa roughly 250,000 years ago (National Human Genome Research
Institute, 2019).

Yet despite the scientific evidence that we are at the DNA level all the
same, that race is not a biological or scientific construct, and that we are all
Africans by origin; race matters. Race although not real is real in its consequences (Duster, 2005). And the Congo is one of those excruciatingly
"silences of history" that humans have inflicted on their fellow human family
that is a case in point of the consequences of racism.

And yet the world we live in—its divisions and conflicts, its widening gap between the rich and poor, its seemingly inexplicable outbursts of violence—is shaped far less by what we celebrate and mythologize than by the painful events we try to forget. Leopold's Congo is but one of those silences of history (Hochschild, King Leopold's Ghost, 1998).

Even more despairing history is that some terrors have been inflicted, or at minimum, condoned or ignored by people of faith. The director of the Human Genome Project, Dr. Francis Collins, is a leading American physician-geneticist and discoverer of disease related genes, recipient of the Presidential Medal of Freedom and a Christian. And his perspective regarding faith and history is as follows:

> … while the long history of religious oppression and hypocrisy is profoundly sobering, the earnest seeker must look beyond the behavior of flawed humans in order to find the truth. Would you condemn an oak tree because its timbers had been used to build battering rams? Would you blame the air for allowing lies to be transmitted through it? Would you judge Mozart's The Magic Flute based on a poorly rehearsed performance by fifth graders? If you had never seen a real sunset over the Pacific, would you allow a tourist brochure as a substitute? Would you evaluate the power of romantic love solely in the light of an abusive marriage next door? No. A real evaluation of the truth of faith depends upon looking at the clean, pure water, not at the rusty containers" (Collins, 2006, p. 30–42).

Rebecca

Race is not only a Black issue, I agree. However, I don't look at race as something to address White people's issues with, but Black people. As a Black woman, I am focused on deconstructing the colonial mindset of Black people and liberating the Black psyche and Black mind. I believe continued blindness is detrimental to a freed Black consciousness, that is why I comment on it so much, and not address the role that White people continue to play in perpetuating racism. I also agree that we are all the same and that racism is a social construct to divide based on economics—to keep the rich, rich and the poor, poor. I also agree that the church has been very complicit in sustaining and enforcing White supremacy rather than challenging it. I think that is why I am so turned off by the church, namely the American church, because they have been mostly silent about it. The White church does not have a monopoly on this either. The Black American church is not guilt-free. That is why although I am a believer, I am hesitant to join a church right now. I listen to podcasts on YouTube about race and awakening the consciousness of the African mind. A channel I really enjoy listening to is that of the late Pastor Steven Darby who really tackles the race issues of America and is all about elevating the Black consciousness so we know who we are, have more self-love, unity with one another, and gain a deeper understanding of the social construction of race and racism.

As a person who grew up in a White home, I never felt self-hatred because of my skin color and how I am perceived as a Black woman in a White dominated world. I never felt less than or inferior because of the color of my skin. However, I do know that my experience is not the same as everyone's and that is why I try to learn and understand other people's experiences and help them understand that they have been programmed to think that way. This mindset is not developed from an internal compass, but an outward manifestation of ideologies that were placed on them to self-subjugation. I am continuously learning and growing because this issue is deeply important to me. It is one of my passions.

References

Ahmad, G. & Awan, M.S., (2017). Colonialism and its socio-political and economic impact. *The Dialogue.* 12(3): 311–320.

Boffey, D. (2018, December 8). Belgium's revamped Africa museum triggers request by DRC. *The Guardian.* https://www.theguardian.com/world/2018/dec/08/belgium-revamped-africa-museum-demands-congo-kabila. Access date February 9, 2019.

Chemi Che-Mponda (2019). http://swahilitime.blogspot.com/2013/02/the-meaning-of-word-mzungu-maana-ya.html. Accessed January 4, 2019.

Collins, F. (2006). *The language of God: A scientist presents evidence for belief.* New York: Simon & Schuster.

Conrad, J. (1996). *Heart of darkness.* Charlottesville, VA: University of Virginia Library.

Del Guidance, P. & Yves, P. (2002). The widespread use of skin lightening creams in Senegal: A persistent health problem in West Africa. *International Journal of Dermatology.* 41(2):69–72.

Duster, T. (2005). Race and reification in Science. *Science* 307(5712): 1050–1051.

Food Agriculture Organization of the United Nations. (2018). The state of food security and nutrition in the world: Building climate resilience for food security and nutrition. http://www.fao.org/3/i9553en/i9553en.pdf

Hochschild, A. (1998). *King Leopold's ghost: A story of greed, terror and heroism in Colonial Africa.* Boston: Houghton Mifflin.

Kendi, I. (2016). *Stamped from the beginning.* New York: Bold Type Books.

Khapoya, V. (1994, P. 99). *The African experience: An introduction.* Englewood Cliffs, NJ: Prentice-Hall.

McCann-Mortimer, P., Augoustinos, M., & LeCouteur, A., (2004). Race and the human genome project: Constructions of scientific legitimacy. *Discourse & Society.* https://doi.org/10.1177%2F0957926504043707

National Human Genome Research Institute https://www.genome.gov

Ngũgĩ wa Thiong'o, (1986). Decolonizing the mind: The politics of language in African literature. Portsmouth, NH: Heinemann Publishing.

Ntshingla, F. (2005, November 27). Women buppies using harmful skin lighteners. *Sunday Times* (South Africa).

Smith, W. D. (1982). European imperialism in the nineteenth and twentieth centuries. NelsonHall.

Snow, J. (2013, October 9). DR Congo: Cursed by its natural wealth. BBC. https://www.bbc.com/news/magazine-24396390

· 9 ·

BEDFORD-STUYVESANT, BROOKLYN

"Women should perceive that the negative attitudes they hold toward their own femaleness are the creation of an antifeminist society, just as the Black shame at being Black was the product of racism. Women should start to replace their negative ideas of their femininity with positive ones affirming their nature more and more strongly.

Shirley Chisholm

Bedford-Stuyvesant (Bed-Stuy), Brooklyn made infamous by Spike Lee's 1989 film, *Do the Right Thing*, has historically had a conflicted reputation for being: diverse, rich with community, a beacon of hope for new immigrants, dangerous, dynamic, segregated, ghettoized, socially progressive and active, and more recently gentrified with both good and bad connotations. What cannot be said about its image is that it is stagnant.

The Dutch originally purchased this north central section of the borough of Brooklyn in 1670 from the Canarsie tribe. This then farmland, derived its name from Peter Stuyvesant the last governor of the New Netherland colony. In the early and mid-19th Century the Brooklyn and Jamaica Railroads were built, and upper- and middle-class German immigrants constructed some of the impressive brownstones and row houses that still stand so majestically today. When Germans moved to the suburbs, working class Irish, Jews,

Italians, and a few English inhabited what is still known today as "a town (borough) of homes and churches." There are 8,800 buildings built before 1900, the largest collection of Victorian architecture in the country. With excellent access to Manhattan and Long Island via Long Island Railroad and the A and C subway lines, its stunning churches, beautifully crafted brownstones, spacious parks, and tree-lined blocks like the award-winning "Greenest Block", Decatur Street, Bed-Stuy was a highly sought after neighborhood for home buyers and renters alike (Bedford-Stuyvesant, Brooklyn History; Helmreich, 2016; Hymowitz, 2017).

The Great Migration

From 1915 to 1970 massive change came to the northern cities of America. Bed-Stuy, along with the rest of New York City, particularly Harlem and the Bronx, were a part of what historians now call The Great Migration, a leaderless, massive, vast, and underreported epic American story (Wilkerson, 2010).

> For six decades, some six million Black southerners left the land of their forefathers and fanned out across the country for an uncertain existence in nearly every other corner of America. The Great Migration would become a turning point in history. It would transform urban America and recast the social and political order of every city it touched. It would force the south to search its soul and finally to lay aside a feudal caste system. It grew out of the unmet promises made after the Civil War and, through the sheer weight of it, helped push the country toward the civil rights revolutions of the 1960s" (Wilkerson, 2010, p. 9).

In Bed-Stuy this mass migration of African Americans from the South came during the Great Depression of the 1930s, progressing a little slower and later than in Manhattan. Southerners came seeking employment, in part due to the decline of agriculture down South and Jim Crow. Some settled first in Harlem and then relocated to Bed-Stuy because it was more affordable and less crowded. Bed-Stuy became a middle- and working-class neighborhood with electric trolleys and the Fulton Street Elevated (later to become the Long Island Railroad) with residents able to commute to Manhattan and downtown Brooklyn. The beautifully constructed brownstones were attractive for home ownership, and like Harlem in Manhattan, Bed-Stuy became a center for Black culture in Brooklyn (Bedford-Stuyvesant, Brooklyn History, 2019). Simultaneously, during the 1930s Caribbean immigrants from Jamaica,

Trinidad, Barbados, Haiti, St. Kitts, Nevis, Grenada, St. Vincent, Antigua, Montserrat, and other islands came to this neighborhood as well.

By the 1970s, the approximately 653 square blocks that make up Bedford-Stuyvesant was an African American enclave and the nation's second largest voluntary Black immigrant community of West Indians. Well over 25% of the residents were homeowners in this architecturally rich community, and the population was an ethnically heterogeneous Black community embracing Blacks with distinct cultural and linguistic backgrounds from the South, the Islands, and increasingly Africa. During the 1970s and 1980s crime and drugs were prevalent, but it has had an exaggerated reputation as an unrelieved slum when in fact it has long been important and significant for strong political, community, and social activism (Woodsworth, 2016).

Joni

Your Dad and I lived in Brooklyn before gentrification from 1978 to 2001, and then I returned to Brooklyn in 2016. During those in between years I always worked in Brooklyn or Queens, but I missed living here. And I now live in Bed-Stuy a few blocks from where I taught school in 1980 when I was 27 years old and had just come to New York with your Dad. We had been married for two years, and I searched for a public-school teaching job not knowing that I would land a job in what was then considered a "bad" neighborhood and a "bad" school. It was not really bad—that was a code word for all Black, although it was chaotic, and some teachers did not have control of their classrooms. But children are children—they wanted to learn; they craved order and adult supervision. If I knew what I know today and with the experience I now have, I could have been a much better teacher.

Bed-Stuy at the time was a high crime neighborhood with neglected and under-funded schools with old textbooks, buildings in disrepair, scared White teachers, and children doing violence toward other children. Children were sometimes scared to go to the bathroom for fear of being beat up or accosted by bullies. Some older teachers were excellent, and some were burnt out. There was a revolving door of teachers mostly first year, inexperienced White teachers, and a general air of chaos. I recall the school administrators tried hard to keep control of the children as Decatur Junior High School #35 had been an excellent school in the past with high standards and good discipline.

But in the early '80s it no longer was. I did my very best to shut my classroom door, to shut out the truant students running the halls and fighting, terrorizing younger students and causing mayhem. I tried very hard to teach—control the discipline in the class, respond to the students. Sometimes I succeeded; sometimes I didn't.

Although I am reluctant to characterize Bed-Stuy at the time as a ghetto or a slum; I will say that it was an almost an all-Black neighborhood where children experienced educational trauma (Schwartz & Schwartz, 2012) to and from school and sometimes in the classrooms. It was a high crime community structurally neglected by the City. It was a segregated school, and I was one of a few White teachers. The children naturally were angry and fearful, and it manifested itself in violence in the halls and the playground. New teachers were sometimes hit or disabused physically or verbally. I won't lie; it was scary driving into work in the morning to Lewis and MacDonough—Junior High School #35. But the problems were due to racist educational policies not the children, community or teachers.

Rebecca

As you have often been one of the only White persons in Black spaces; I have often been the only Black person in White environments. Sometimes in the past I felt more

Figure 9.1   Graduation NYU – Mom and Dad

comfortable in White areas than in Black areas. African Americans who have never been around White people may experience fear and discomfort. Let me be clear, however; I don't try to act a certain way to appeal to White people—like a model minority. I hate that. You need to be who you are and practice your culture --who you are.

Joni

As a child, I think the first time I knew I was White was when a girlfriend on the block brought a Black baby doll for us to play with. We played baby dolls all the time, but they were always White. This day was different. I was intrigued and as a small child, I already knew color but perhaps that's the day I knew I was White. Whites don't have to know they are White because of White supremacy and it is normalized in this society. We don't have to deal with race especially if we continue to maintain life primarily in all White settings. I am not exceptional, but I have lived, worked, and engaged in diverse and non-White environments the bulk of my adult life. This doesn't make me better or special, but it in some ways makes my life experience different from some Whites. It frames everything I am and do.

Rebecca

Your racial experiences are in some ways the inverse of mine. Until more recently, my formative years were primarily in White settings—my family and my high school. I was one of two Black students at Fontbonne Hall Academy, an all-White girls Catholic High School in Bay Ridge, Brooklyn. So, when I went there it helped my mindset to be with the White girls. It was a good school. I remember Sister Anne; she tried to work with me, and she didn't have to. Sis Anne was sweet but strict. I thrived in that White school—intellectually and socially. There are so many good memories.

One is with my Dad, the Father/Daughter Dance. My White Dad and his Black daughter. We almost won the dance contest my sophomore year. But instead we came in second place, the judges gave it to this father who was differently abled; I think they were trying to be nice to him. Only just a few girls went, so I bonded with Claire Jacobs, her father was nice to me—her father died of cancer recently and I saw it on Facebook and sent her my condolences, letting her know that I will always remember him for being a kind man. You don't forget those types of kindnesses.

Resident Social Activism

It is sometimes thought that the Civil Rights Movement only took place in the South. But Northern cities were battlegrounds, too. New York, and specifically Bed-Stuy through the Brooklyn chapter of the Congress of Racial Equality (CORE) battled discrimination in housing, employment and education. Activists worked to integrate schools, improve sanitation, and create jobs (Tuttle, 2016). Resident community activists were a significant force in these struggles despite the neighborhoods increasing crime and drugs in the 70s and 80s.

Although the image of this neighborhood has been and sometimes still is described as a ghetto, the truth is that this neighborhood was not just abandoned to crime and poverty as so many narratives lead one to believe. Instead, there is a counternarrative of an ongoing fight for integrated civil rights and Black power with community self-determination through the decades. This is complex history and includes a dynamic range of local Black activists (Dougherty, 2004, p. 107). Crime and violence were high at this time all over the country, and Bed-Stuy was not an exception. But it was not only inhabited by criminals, and victims of violence, nor was it only a space of poverty and unsafety. Community members developed Block watcher programs in the 1970s and 80s, working with police to keep the neighborhood safe.

The War on Poverty, a federal government program of established in 1964 and 1965 under President Lyndon Johnson, created Medicare, Medicaid, food stamps, Job Corps, VISTA, Head Start, and Title 1 Education initiatives aimed to eradicate poverty. Some of these programs are still operative and history has shown poverty, if not eradicated, has lessened.

Unfortunately, other effects were that the War on Poverty pathologized places like Bed-Stuy and tried to fix places of high poverty through policing and prisons rather than make the institutional, systemic, and structural changes necessary to eradicate poverty itself. Bed-Stuy residents had strong agency and homeowner activism working for change throughout the 70s, 80s and 90s (Woodsworth, 2016).

Women of Color have historically led the way; activists such as Elsie Richardson, highlighted in Woodsworth's *Battle for Bed-Stuy* who in the mid-sixties fought to define her neighborhood as a "community, not a ghetto." According to Woodsworth, Black women activists through the 60s and on into the 70s and 80s shaped, sustained, and preserved Bed-Stuy bolstering it against the gentrification we see today. So, yes, there has been and continues to be a protracted War on Poverty in this community shouldered in many ways by long term grassroots activism led by Black women who perform activist mothering—cross-generational community work developed from a mothering role (Woodsworth, 2016; Naples, 1992). One of the most famous and influential of these women was Shirley Chisholm.

Shirley Chisholm

Perhaps it is the habitus created by spaces like Bed-Stuy that generate so many well-known celebrities, artists, sports icons, writers, politicians, and activists. Bed-Stuy seems to have an unusually high number of famous people who were raised in its streets: Jackie Gleason, Lena Horne, Jackie Robinson, Floyd Patterson, Bobby Fischer, Jay Z, Norah Jones, Chris Rock, Frank McCourt, Juan Williams, Lenny Wilkens, June Jordan, Biggie Smalls, Lil Kim, Barbara Streisand, Judge Judy, Mike Tyson, Spike Lee, and Shirley Chisholm.

In the 1970s, Shirley Anita Chisholm (1924–2005) was an American politician, educator, and author. She was the first Black woman elected to the US Congress, representing New York's 12th District which at the time included Bed-Stuy, serving seven terms from 1969–1983. She was also the first Black and first woman to attempt a run for president of the US, announcing her presidential nomination at The Concord Baptist Church in her beloved Bed-Stuy. She was born in Bed-Stuy in 1924; her father was from British Guiana and her mother from Barbados. She attended primary school in Barbados and Girls' High School on Nostrand Avenue in Bed-Stuy then was a graduate of Brooklyn College (Chisholm, 2010).

Chisolm's activism included a wide range of targets; she fought hard for unemployment benefits for domestic workers, maternity rights for teachers, access to childcare, legalization of abortion, and education initiatives such as the still influential SEEK (Search for Education, Elevation and Knowledge) program at the City University of New York which continues to give opportunities to low-income students to enroll and be supported in college. In addition, she spoke out against the Vietnam War early in her career voting against military spending. She was always a strong proponent of equality for women, hiring all women for her office, half of whom were African American. She was the founder of the Congressional Black Caucus and the National Women's Political Caucus (Chisholm, 2010). In terms of race and women's rights, she was ahead of her time. Her words ring as true today as they did in her day:

Unless we start to fight and defeat the enemies in our own country, poverty and racism, and make our talk of equality and opportunity ring true, we are exposed in the eyes of the world as hypocrites when we talk about making people free" (Chisholm, 2010, p. 112–113).

Much of the hypocrisy of Americans on the subject of race seems to be unconscious. Perhaps self-deception would be a better word for it. Racism is so universal in this country, so widespread and deep-seated, that it is invisible because it is so normal (p. 147).

The civil rights movement of the 1950s and early 1960s—the movement was a failure. Everyone who was deeply involved in it hates to admit that (Chisholm, 2010, p.149).

What most Whites think of when they say "ghetto" is a Black slum. To them, all Black communities are alike—rundown, crime-ridden jungles. When Blacks use the word "ghetto" they almost always prefix it with "so-called", to reject this White stereotype (Chisholm, 2010, p. 152).

The accuracy of her thinking seems so woefully relevant in the 21st Century, and we can only hope that when she says, "White America is beginning to be able to admit that it carries racial prejudice in its heart, and that understanding marks the beginning of the end of racism," (p. 175) that she is correct. Her fight for racial equality was only paralleled in effort and intensity by her fight for women's rights. In her own words:

It is not female egotism to say that the future of mankind may very well be ours to determine. It is a fact. The warmth, gentleness, and compassion that are part of the female stereotype are positive human values, values that are becoming more and more important as the values of our world begin to shatter and fall from our grasp. The strength of Christ, Gandhi, and Martin Luther King was a strength of gentleness, understanding, and compassion with no element of violence in it. It was, in short, a female strength, and that is the kind that often marks the highest type of man (Chisholm, 2010, p. 178).

Shirley wanted to be remembered as a woman who fought for change in the 20th century (Lynch, 2004), and she equated women's fight for equality with the fight for equality of Black people. She combined these two struggles, and this would be her legacy.

Rebecca

Yes, like Shirley Chisholm, I want to have and leave a legacy. I don't want to just live the status quo; it is so easy to be a follower, not rocking the boat. When I have rocked the boat, I became the enemy, I stopped being liked on the job.

When I stood up for what I believed in, I noticed that in this past job that I was no longer the token Black that the organization loved; their darling, Black girl. I have a big personality; I can do something. I am one of those Black people that White people love to love.

Africans look at race differently. Africans, for the most part, revere foreigners especially, Whites. Whites and all westerners are more esteemed than in America. That is the mindset. So, as an expat and westerner, I benefit from this. When in Africa I benefited from this mindset of White supremacy because I am a foreigner and a US citizen. I know as a Black woman I interview very well. Living in the US and being "woke" or aware is hard. My eyes are now open that this stuff is out there.

Joni

Shirley Chisholm was a strong, Black woman and you are, too. She announced her presidency just a few blocks from where I live now, down Marcy Avenue. It's amazing to think there is such history flowing through this neighborhood. Looking at photos of Shirley Chisholm, I notice her gap, and lisp. It makes me think of your gap, although her gap was no way as attractive as yours in my estimation. Chisholm's gap was on the side of her mouth; yours was between your front two teeth, and you did not have a lisp at all. I loved your gap; I always thought it made you unique and cute.

You no longer have it. You had a dental retainer to remove it. I get it; you didn't want to be cute but to be a grown woman. But I miss your gap. I miss in some ways the little girl you were. I only have one photo of you as a baby in the orphanage; all other photos are from nine years old when you were adopted. I lost those baby years—that is a loss for me. Now, I miss the little girl, and the loss of the gap reminds me of that.

Don't get me wrong. We now have an adult mother-daughter relationship, and it is fine and growing and wonderful in every way. The gap is gone in our relationship as well. The relationship is reciprocal now; it is rational and emotional, and I feel closer to you than ever.

Rebecca

I am a strong-willed woman, and I want to have a voice. I can't keep quiet when I see injustice. I must be true to myself. I need to stand up against racism, but how do I negotiate all of this? Then there is another issue. I want to embrace the feminine side of me.

I like the idea of being taken care of—no apologies. I want a partner, someone behind me. I know my limitations as a woman. I want a man to come home to—I want that emotional support. I want more than a companion and a partner; I want a soulmate.

I have had to take care of myself; be masculine in many senses of the word. Now I want to embrace the feminine. The Bible says "it is not good for man to be alone."I don't think it is good for me to be alone. I have had several men who would marry me in a heartbeat, but I didn't feel the same way. I don't want to compromise. I am a survivor. I always rise.

I am still trying to find my way and figure things out. Sometimes these issues of race and gender really wear you down. I wonder how I might step in and help and integrate and be part of solutions. I'm here for a purpose. I have had these life experiences and adoption for a purpose. What is my legacy? What is my purpose? How do I live my life to leave something behind?

Black Land Matters

Bedford-Stuyvesant is in the process of gentrification, but it is not "coming back" as some say because it never went anywhere. Fortunately, it is one of the few neighborhoods in Brooklyn where the residents have had a hand in its gentrification. The community has a long history of Black home ownership dating back to 1838, before the Civil War when James Weeks purchased land in the now Bed-Stuy and Crown Heights sections of Brooklyn. This was eleven years after the abolition of slavery. Freed People of Color created Weeksville, a Black community of 500 residents in a 16-block area which became a sanctuary for its residents. They built a whole cooperative and self-sustaining community with stores, a newspaper, barber shops, schools and churches (Weeksville Heritage Center, 2019).

Buying and keeping land matters in a democracy and was tied to the right to vote. Therefore, these far-sighted Black landowners and investors, for a price, were able to vote along with Whites males. Four houses remain and have been preserved, and it is now the Weeksville Heritage Center; it is an historic landmark.

Despite its historic legacy of home ownership, Bed-Stuy is a contested frontier of gentrification so organizations like Black Land Matters work to support the process of stewardship and connectivity to the land and land ownership. How do you keep land? What is the land value and succession plan so that Blacks keep land for longer than one or two generations? With the prospectors in Bed-Stuy, these are crucial questions that relate to social activism in response to gentrification—the process of repairing and rebuilding deteriorating mostly urban neighborhoods resulting in the poor being pushed out with an influx of middle and affluent often White people. Behind social movements there needs to be cooperative financial movements. Land is power and a vehicle for the accumulation of wealth and self-determination (Lewis, 2017). Having land is central to the role in the liberation of Black people. Bed-Stuy seems positioned better than other neighborhoods like Williamsburg to have a hand in continued Black land ownership thus monitoring gentrification. From 1990 to 2014 went up rents went up 36.1% (Hairston, 2018) making it difficult for the working class and poor to stay, and when the recession hit in 2008 many family owned Bed-Stuy properties were lost to foreclosure

In addition, the 2010 US Census Bureau data reports that 30.7% of Bed-Stuy residents were in poverty with increases in the number of low-income residents while the increase in high income residents also increased along racial lines. Income disparity and inequality is on display in this neighborhood and gentrification has played some role although there has long been lingering poverty in Bed-Stuy.

To be fair, gentrification is a mixed bag. There is positive impact for some along with negative results for others (Grossett, 2014). With gentrification comes improved streets with fixed potholes, trendy coffee shops, more police presence, emergence of new businesses, and fresh fruits and vegetables. But this can be at the extreme expense of pushing out and displacing long-time residents, increased homelessness, loss of ethnic identity and history, and the disruption of community bonds. This is no small cost.

Then there is rebranding which may be the most insidious part because of what it does to the heart and soul of communities. Rebranding is not just raising rents and home prices but erasing the history and presence of the existing neighborhood and its residents. According to US representative Hakeem Jeffries, "Neighborhoods have a history, culture and character that should not be tossed overboard whenever a realtor decides it would be easier to market under another name" (Buckley, 2011). Rebranding or not, what cannot be ignored or disputed; change has come to Brooklyn once again.

Rebecca

I think Brooklyn now is a little bit better. When Black people are in a neighborhood there is a certain sort of aliveness and energy. So, in Bed–Stuy Blacks are still there

although there are more Whites now, and I think it is nice now with the Black flavor but more options, restaurants, cleaner, things to do and safer.

In terms of me, I like how I am in the world. I can go to a White neighborhood and I can be ok. I can go in a Black neighborhood and I can feel ok. I can be in a nice place and feel that I fit in. I like the ability to traverse in these kinds of ethnic and racial spheres.

In terms of Black and White spaces, one Black person seems to be ok in a group of Whites, but when there are several or a group of People of Color, this often is more of a threat to Whites. I have heard stuff like that with Black and White groups congregating and who is welcome and who is not. I don't know; maybe it is true that People of Color are a perceived threat.

I want to buy land. I know that is important particularly for me as a Black woman. You and I have talked about doing it together. It makes sense; we need land that will make us powerful and secure. This is one of my life goals to be a land and property owner.

Joni

I'm not sure that I think Brooklyn is "better"—that is a coded word—better for whom, at what costs: social, cultural and financial? Brooklyn has changed so much. I have very mixed feelings about gentrification. I hate the poor being displaced and priced out of their homes. I hate the loss of community and culture. I hate being the gentrifier or gentry as I move back to the Brooklyn I love. But I do admit I enjoy the new cafes, restaurants, trendy shops, fixed potholes, and picked up garbage.

I still love Brooklyn and Bed-Stuy is just right for me. It's a mix of all the elements of life I value—warm people, diverse population and cultures, small businesses, bodegas, restaurants, easy access by public transportation to Manhattan, my West African dance class, the Long Island Railroad to see my grandkids. There is art, beautiful architecture, especially churches, music, museums, libraries, my college, and friends—all within easy reach. My apartment is a small floor space with big windows and a skylight—lots of light overlooking several huge trees so the birds wake me up and nest near my windows. It is airy, quiet, and sunny with high ceilings. Bed-Stuy provides a rich, stimulating, and friendly spot for me to heal, change, and rebrand myself.

Rebecca

The changes in the last couple of years have propelled me into adulthood. Before I was thinking as a child. Now I see myself thinking as an adult. Probably because *of living in other countries, having the responsibility of Country Director in Uganda, your divorce from Dad, and living by myself propelled the evolution in me. I had to learn to be an adult and take care of myself. It just sort of clicked in my brain and my body that this is what I have to do. I don't have the desire to go out and party anymore, I'd rather stay home and read, study, watch informational programming on my computer. This happened since the Congo.*

I think aging is not the same as maturity. Now that I am nearing my 40s, I feel like I need to live life on purpose, maximize my gifts, talents, and abilities. I don't want to waste my life. I met a man in Uganda who owns ten businesses, started a hospital; he uses science and technology in his businesses. One example is that he has brought in vitro fertilization to Uganda. He has his kids working for him. One son oversees a fleet of cars, another oversees a business that produces honey in the bush and exports millions of crates of honey from the bush to Europe and abroad. Honey and bees are a global trade and a low capital business for African entrepreneurs. With profits, he is feeding and providing excess products to school children. Another son is growing food for export and with the excess food, he feeds school children in need (Mr. Richard Lolobo, personal communication, July, 2019). He is revolutionizing his country. You should hear his story. It is so inspiring.

This is what I want to do—give everything, live intentionally, own property, be self-sufficient, and own my own business, give profits to others. I want to leave a legacy like this man and Shirley Chisholm.

Joni

Beyond the change of being back in Brooklyn, my life has majorly evolved in the last four years because of my divorce from your father. Of course, it was the hardest decision of my life, but I have lived authentically, honestly, and that is good. I think my relationship with you has also evolved and—may I dare say—matured. I feel like we now relate as adults not so much child and parent. That feels right and appropriate.

I came across a couple of quotes that really ring true to me: "Intelligence is the ability to adapt to change" (Strauss, 2018) and "The ability to adapt to change is an indication of maturity." That sounds about right to me. I like aging. I can say I have great joy in growing older. I have fallen in love, invested once again in my teaching, I write every day, I read books, and I dance, drink wine, chat with friends, spoil my grandchildren, pray and meditate, and have think time. Most days I live in the present moment. I like to think "I laugh at the future" (Proverbs, 31:25, English

Standard Version). *And one of my best joys is watching you and following you as you journey through life.*

References

Bedford-Stuyvesant, Brooklyn (History) (2019). Urbanareas.net. https://urbanareas.net/info/resources/neighborhoods-brooklyn/bedford-stuyvesant-brooklyn-history/. Accessed: December 10, 2019.

Buckley, C. (2011, April 20). ProCro, SoBro, FiDi, BoCoCa: A Lawmaker says, 'Enough.' *The New York Times*.

Chisholm, S. (2010). *Unbought and unbossed*. Boston: Houghton Mifflin.

Dougherty, J. (2004). *More than one struggle*. Chapel Hill, NC: The University of North Carolina Press.

Grossett, N. (Producer) (2014), The shifting faces of Bedford-Stuyvesant: Mini documentary Youtube.com/watch?v=LEmPgcMCZql. Accessed: December 10, 2019.

Hairston, K. (2018, December 21). The truth behind gentrification in Bed-Stuy. https://medium.com/@kashief.hairston/the-truth-behind-gentrification-in-bed-stuy-6b20. Accessed: December 10, 2019.

Helmrich, W. (2016). The Brooklyn nobody knows: An urban walking tour. Princeton, NJ: Princeton University Press.

Hymowitz, K., (2017, June 28). The blossoming of Bed-Stuy: Is gentrification racist? The Bridge: Brooklyn Business News. https://thebridgebk.com/blossoming-bed-stuy-gentrification-racist/. Accessed: December 10, 2019.

Lewis, K. (2017, February 24). *Black* land and its role in the liberation of Black people. *Huffington Post*.

Lynch, S. (Producer) (2004). Chisholm '72: Unbought & Unbossed, USA: Realside Productions.

Naples, N. (1992). Activist mothering: Cross-generational continuity in the community work of women from low-income urban neighborhoods. *Gender and Society*. 6(3): 441–463.

Schwartz, J. & Schwartz, P. (Producers). (2012). A new normal: Young men of color, trauma and engagement in learning. (Videotape & YouTube). New York: University of New York Cultural Diversity Project.

Strauss, V. (2018, March 29). Stephen Hawking famously said, "Intelligence is the ability to adapt to change. But did he really say it? *Washington Post*. https://www.washingtonpost.com/news/answer-sheet/wp/2018/03/29/stephen-hawking-famously-said-intelligence-is-the-ability-to-adapt-to-change-but-did-he-really-say-it/?utm_term=.afd8fb0a4f97. Accessed: December 10, 2019.

Tuttle, L. (2016, October 25) Civil rights in Brooklyn. https://www.mcny.org/story/civil-rights-brooklyn

Weeksville Heritage Center (2019) https://www.weeksvillesociety.org. Accessed: December 10, 2019.

Wilkerson, I. (2010). *The warmth of other suns: The epic story of America's great migration.* New York: Random House.

Woodsworth, M. (2016). *Battle for Bed-Stuy: The long war on poverty in New York City.* Boston: Harvard University Press.

· 1 0 ·

THE YELLOW DRESS

"I believe that each work of art, whether it is a work of great genius, or something
very small, comes to the artist and says, "Here I am. Enflesh me. Give birth to me.""
Madeleine L'Engle, Walking on Water

Rebecca

*Returning from Africa after another year in the field, my plane landed at John
F. Kennedy Airport in New York and the consulate said to me as he stamped my
passport, "Welcome Home!" God, those words sounded so good, especially when
you don't know where home is yet.*

Joni

*The yellow dress startled me. I spied it in a fitting room three-way mirror at
Joyce Leslie Women's Shop. Its effect was immediate, like the scent of a potent
perfume that takes you back to a different time and place. It was a women's
size 10, an Asian style, very womanly with a high collar and three embroidered
buttons. The fit was slim and contoured, but not provocative. She tried on other*

dresses but would choose the pale yellow. This reflection took me back to the first yellow dress.

I wondered if she remembered it, too, if she remembered the October morning that we left the orphanage. That morning I packed my items which included an ebony cutting board, matching salad forks, a sculptured, smooth, wood pitcher all handmade by an 80-year-old Haitian gentleman in his workshop among the palm trees. My dresses, sandals, bathrobe, toothbrush, books, comb, makeup, presents for Paul and the boys were packed into two sky blue suitcases.

Rebecca packed nothing that morning. Instead an orphanage worker, Yvrose, took Rebecca's wrist and led her to a locked closet. While Yvrose unfastened the padlock, Rebecca stood motionless. Other children appeared and formed a crowd in front of this mysterious closet. The closet doors opened upon a row of multi-colored girls dresses and boys dress suits. The children's eyes stared at this almost magical sight.

Rebecca stood still for a long while until she pointed to a red-laced party frock, a green velvet one, and a pale yellow. Yvrose muttered something in Creole under her breath and pulled the three dresses from the closet, locking the door behind her. The red, green and yellow were displayed on one of the army cots used for the children's dormitory beds. The children encircled the cot to view the choice, perhaps fantasizing about the day they would choose an outfit from the closet.

Yvrose held the red frock up against Rebecca and spoke sharply; something negative. Rebecca then looked at the green for a long time and shook her head "no." She finally chose the yellow for her homecoming. It had a White sleeveless bodice with a yellow pleated skirt. There was a matching polyester yellow jacket giving the dress the appearance of quality. Perhaps it had belonged to an American girl, given to her by grandparents as a birthday gift, and she had outgrown this children's size 8. The family had then donated the dress, and now it hung with the other fancy second-hand items.

Yvrose plaited Rebecca's hair in tight braids that stretched her scalp, then tied satin yellow ribbons all over her head. She wore white anklets inside her slightly scuffed white patent leather shoes, and her bare legs had bruises from falls on the concrete play area. She scrutinized my every move that morning, as if she thought I might leave without her.

I was tired. The night had been hot with Rebecca sleeping scrunched against me in my single cot. She insisted upon sleeping with me rather than in her own bed. Her warm body next to mine made me hotter and stickier, but I wanted to hold her even if it was uncomfortable. I caressed her head and hair and examined her sleeping face as if she were a baby rather than a nine-year-old.

Unable to sleep, I envisioned how hard it might be for her to leave her friends. Unfortunately, we couldn't discuss the leave-taking. We couldn't tackle a compli-cated conversation about feelings, even though she did understand some English. I couldn't make out the Creole she spoke with the other children, as they laughed and pointed at me or when she stole a glimpse at me.

After all, this had been her family since birth. Maybe in the end she wouldn't want to leave, I thought looking down at her sleeping face nestled in the crook of my arm. Would I have to tear her away? How would she say good-bye to ten-year-old Bernadette her companion since birth?

Bernadette was the orphanage bully. She was built like a football player, much bigger than Rebecca, and was always in trouble. Rebecca seemed to be a close accomplice and was no pushover either. How would she leave Lissette, the quietest of the group? I imagined Lissette as the one with whom Rebecca shared her confidences.

That morning Rebecca ate nothing. I ate cornmeal with herring or "black fish" as Mom Workman called this Haitian dish and drank sweet passion fruit juice. The leave-taking I expected did not happen. There was no crying, hugging, kissing not even a good-bye to the children and workers. At least, I did not see it. Perhaps it had taken place before that morning, in private. I don't know. Leaving the orphan-age for America, there was no suitcase, no duffel bag, no stuffed animal, not even a brown paper bag filled with childhood treasures. Only the yellow dress she wore on her back.

We loaded the dusty red Chevy van with my two suitcases and jumped in, sit-ting in the backseat. The driver, Michael, an American missionary asked Rebecca if she wanted to drive to the front of the orphanage and say her good-byes. In Creole, she told him "no" she had already said good-bye. Michael asked again, just to make sure he heard her right. She again said, "No, I am ready to go." The look on Michael's face betrayed his surprise that someone leaving the home of their whole life wouldn't want to say a last good-bye. But Rebecca's resolve told him she just wanted to leave.

Driving through the poverty that is Port-au-Prince and Carrefour, Rebecca sat resolute. Her head and shoulders stood erect and her eyes looked straight forward. She never looked back. There would be time for looking back later. There would be time to make sense of the years at the orphanage. But driving on the way to the airport that morning was not that time. We purposely arrived at the airport three hours early because you couldn't anticipate what immigration procedures you might be subject to and how long they would take. I didn't want to take any chances.

We spoke very little. We were both anxious to board the plane. She sat quietly in a badly cracked orange plastic airport chair resplendent in her yellow dress. From my purse, I brought out crayons and a coloring book, but she didn't seem interested. She ate the M & M's I gave her, fingering each one slowly and stared straight ahead. The airport buzzed with noise increasing with the heat of the day. There was no air conditioning. As the one afternoon flight from Miami to Port-au-Prince landed and released its passengers, people scurried to the baggage claim area nearly fighting for their luggage. Passengers arriving from America collected mounds of luggage closed with belts, ropes, and twine. They brought back American goods for their relatives; items not available in Haiti. I was restless, concerned that something would go wrong, that we wouldn't pass customs, that some technicality would stop Rebecca from boarding the plane. For three long hours we waited.

Then we saw American pilots striding toward boarding gate #3; our gate. One of them, the captain perhaps, a tall graying man saw Rebecca. "Is this your first time flying?" he asked bending down to her. She shook her head yes and smiled shyly. Maybe it was the yellow dress and the ribbons or her beautiful face, but all three pilots couldn't help but smile. "Are you going to America?" another pilot said. Again, she nodded and smiled.

When a flight attendant announced our flight, I took Rebecca's hand. The minute Rebecca saw others moving she steered me to the gate and nearly pulled me to the plane. Our seats were in the middle, and we settled in. The plane was only about half full. I fastened her seatbelt and settled back for the ride. Rebecca observed everything.

It was dark when we approached New York. A clear night, we saw the millions of lights of this immigrant city. As the plane landed at JFK, she squealed with delight. Just as the wheels hit the runway, the Haitian passengers let out a cry of "Praise the Lord", "Hallelujah" and clapped their hands. Rebecca joined in.

We unloaded and then were herded to customs. We stood on a long line that snaked around a half dozen poles and waited for our documents to be checked. Once through this checkpoint, we were directed to another room where we waited for another two hours to have our documents checked again. At each checkpoint, I held my breath thinking something would be missing or something in error. I couldn't forget that the adoption was not finalized, and the Social Welfare in Haiti had not wanted to let her go.

Our adoption was a Haitian adoption not an American one which meant that the court finalization proceedings had to be completed in Haiti. If the adoption was an American one, finalization would take place in the US. Under ordinary circumstances, children are not allowed out of a country if their foreign adoption is not finalized. We left with a permanent visa but an incomplete adoption. This was unheard of in adoption circles at that time. I knew that God had orchestrated this adoption although my faith was weak at times and fear nearly overwhelmed me. We were not doing anything wrong—Rebecca was an orphan with no birth parents to be found, and we had all documentation completed and approved; however, the Haitian government was slow to process anything in its corrupted state.

While waiting in one immigration room, we heard a woman shouting in Creole to an immigration official. She needed an interpreter and one was found. The interpreter had trouble understanding the woman as she ranted and raved, but finally the story was told. It appeared as if her passport was suspect, perhaps forged, and we were all onlookers to this spectacle.

Finally, we made it through; Rebecca's green card would come in the mail in a few weeks. I nearly kissed the immigration agent at this news. It was nearly 9 pm, and we had been traveling since early morning. I grabbed Rebecca's hand and ran toward the exit. I couldn't wait to see Nathan, Matthew and Paul. I knew Paul was worried and wondering where we were. In those days, there were no cell phones. We walked down a long corridor following the exit arrows when suddenly the corridor opened into a large crowded lobby.

I saw Paul's tall 6'1" frame and Nathan and Matthew in the back searching for us. In their little hands, the boys held presents for their new sister. I steered Rebecca toward her new family. She walked straight past them; her eyes afraid to make contact. Paul caught her and bent down to kiss her. The boys timidly pushed the little dolls into her hands. "This is for you," they shyly said. She took them with no response.

At home there was a handmade sign, "Welcome Home, Rebecca" plus chocolate cake and rocky road ice cream that we could hardly eat because of fatigue. We took quick photos to capture the moment and undressed her and put the pale-yellow dress on a hanger.

She never wore the dress again. She outgrew it. In the days, months and years that followed I wished so desperately that she could outgrow the past the way she outgrew the yellow dress. But it wasn't so. The past had a way of staying with her, even though she tried to rid herself of it by not saying good-bye, and by keeping her eyes and head erect and straight—not looking back.

In another closet the yellow dresses hang next to one another, crowded between skirts, blouses and dresses of a teenager. When searching the closet for one of my missing sweaters, I spot them –the dress of a little girl and of a very young woman. When decluttering and cleaning, I will never choose to put them in a plastic bag to send to another orphanage. The first dress will never be a hand-me-down again and the second one will have only one owner.

Figure 10.1   First week home

Rebecca

I don't remember the yellow dress incident. I don't think that the closet you describe was a closet; I remember it to be a drawer. In the drawer were ribbons and bows and fancy things, and you are right; I remember it was locked. The main thing I remember about the day I left Haiti was the airplane ride. I remember feeling the uplift of the plane and how my stomach was tickled causing me to laugh. I was ready to go. I have never been that kind of person even as a kid to be quiet, so I find it unlikely that I was so quiet.

I remember while waiting for you to adopt me receiving your letters and the plush animals. I don't know if I received everything you sent because Mom Workman had a bunch of boxes up in her residence area, boxes of unopened toys that I guess were sent for the children. For some reason, either due to my personality or because I was the only child who could speak sentences in English, I was treated specially. I could go up to the administrative offices or Mom Workman's residence and hang around the adults, Mom Workman, Elsie, a Haitian missionary, and Karen, a White administrator. I guess it was kind of like stealing, but I went into the boxes, and I brought items down to the other children. The toys were just there so I figured I'd distribute them; no one ever said anything.

Mom Workman died a few years ago, and I heard that Karen lost a lot of weight and had a son. Elsie, I saw recently, and she looked tired. She's in her late 70s now, and she looked good. She always wanted to marry. People should not give up the God-given desire for marriage, love and companionship. I don't think it is natural for people to be alone. You need other people around you. It grooms you. I live with people; roommates. We need that to evolve and learn how to be with people.

Around the time of the adoption, there was a lot of stuff going on at the orphanage. It was becoming uncomfortable for us girls who were pre-pubescent. There was some sexual bullying by some of the boys, so it was a good time for me to leave. I was starting to get uncomfortable with the boys and one of the missionary men. Even though this was a Christian orphanage and the motives were good and a great deal of good was done, not everything was good for the children.

American Christians and Adoption

American White Christians have long been involved in adoptions often framed as "child rescue." Unfortunately, some Christians do not have a critical understanding of adoption as an industry fueled by Western demand and money and promoted as a "White savior complex." This naivety sometimes ignores the orphan's existing families, cultures and blinds the need for institutional redresses to poverty and racism (Joyce, 2013).

As mentioned previously, between 1854 and 1929 approximately 100,000–250,000 children from mostly poor immigrant Catholic and Jewish families in New York City were transported by Orphan Train to Midwest Protestant homes. Then from the 1950s through 1970s another child saving project, the Child Welfare League of America's Indian Adoption Project relocated 25 to 35 % of all Native American children from reservations to White American homes. Some of the children were formally adopted; some were taken into foster care. Others were raised in orphanages. This was an attempt at assimilation.

In the end, due to protest and lobbying on behalf of Native Americans a restriction of Native American children from being adopted outside of their culture and community was put into place. The Indian Child Welfare Act in 1978 prohibits and restricts adoption of Native American children outside of their community (National Indian Law Library).

These two domestic adoption movements, Orphan Trains and the Indian Adoption Project, engaged Protestant evangelism and American assimilation in large measure. Then as also referred to previously, in 1955 the saving of children through adoption went international with Harry and Bertha Holt and Korea's Amerasian war orphans. These children were bi-racial offspring of Korean mothers and US or British soldiers during and after the Korean War. The Holt Evangelical Mission is in existence today and is often credited with being the spearhead for international adoptions overall (Herman, 2012).

Baby Scoop Era

In terms of domestic adoptions, from 1945 to 1973 an estimated 4 million children were placed in adoption in the US. This boom in baby placements was caused by an increase in premarital pregnancies resulting from the liberalization of sexual mores and restrictions on birth control. Babies born out of wedlock were termed illegitimate, and the mothers often considered psychologically deviant, and sinful. If they were unable to support their child alone, they were counseled to give their babies up for adoption. Unwed mothers were sent to maternity homes which served as conduits for adoptive parents (Ellison, 2003; Petrie, 1998). Maternity homes and agencies used coercion and the stigma of premarital pregnancy to force unwed mothers into relinquishing their babies to infertile couples (MusingsofaBirthmom.com, 2014)). The birthmothers essentially became invisible. First mothers, a term used by many women instead of birthmothers, (Davenport, 2010) would in most cases lose complete contact with their babies.

During the 1960s–1990s, most evangelical Christian churches turned their backs on social justice causes and although there were a few adoptions by families within this tradition, it was mostly forgotten and abandoned. The reasons for this are unclear but after the active participation of the Holt eras at its height, the church appears less involved and more centered on personal salvation and not social gospel issues.

The Evangelical Adoption Movement

This changed around 2004, when Jedd Medefind's Christian Alliance for Orphans gained momentum with the support of Rick Warren and his Saddleback Church as well as *Focus on the Family* through their *Wait No More Program* out of Colorado Springs, Colorado. Evangelicals no longer wanted to only care about babies in the womb, prolife and anti-abortion; but desired to take on the issues of the child after birth through adoption and foster care. The two movements, adoption and anti-abortion, dove tailed. Jedd Medefind became the White House Faith-based Initiatives Director in 2008 which further propelled this adoption movement (Joyce, 2013).

From 2008 forward, evangelical conferences on orphan care flourished: books were written, international adoptions increased, and thousands of churches across the country held *Orphan Sundays*. Warren's *Saddleback Church, the Southern Baptists, Bethany Christian Services*, and *Christian Alliance for Orphans* were at the forefront. Located mostly in the Midwest and West these White churches supported an estimated 20,000 international adoptions into American families. Many families adopted multiple children of all ages and both genders. This was in some minds a fuller expression of pro life. Most were admirable and well-meaning people who wanted to save children twice—first physically and then spiritually. Movement leaders developed an *orphan theology*; the theology links the Biblical concept of spiritual adoption by God to physical adoption. As believers become part of God's family, children become part of a new family (Joyce, 2013). Christian Alliance for Orphans is still operative today, hosting national conferences every year (Christian Alliance for Orphans, https://cafo.org/summit/).

The Evangelical Adoption Movement under Scrutiny

Unfortunately, this is not the entire story, international adoption is a multi-billion-dollar industry. In poor countries the opportunity for corruption is pervasive as children can become a commodity sought after by intermediaries and agencies for economic gain. There are troubling realities of stolen children, coercion of mothers and unethical recruitment methods used to deceive both birth parents and adoptive parents. Often, it may simply be a cultural misunderstanding of what adoption really means, but sometimes child trafficking and adoptions can be connected. As a result of these realities of international adoptions in poor countries, the Evangelical Adoption Movement has come under criticism (Crary, 2013).

The first criticism is that the movement has often closed its eyes to adoption-related fraud, trafficking, child laundering, kidnapping and purchase of infants. The second criticism is that instead of adoption, the movement ought to embrace alternatives to poverty, providing family support to keep children in their own countries with their own families. Another criticism is the view of adoptive parents as saviors or rescuers. In many ways the concept of interest convergence (Bell, 1980) comes into play. The White adopters seem to be doing an altruistic act by adopting a needy child when in fact the adopters stand to benefit the most and are doing it for their own interests: having a baby and family, feeling noble, assuaging guilt or addressing the racial problem (Associated Press, 2015).

The numbers used to promote this movement are also problematic. In 2011, the movement stated there was a global orphan crisis—143 million orphans and growing; this number was taken from the UN's tally of orphaned and vulnerable children (Joyce, 2013). But these numbers are not real. Most of the children in the 143 million live with a single parent or extended family in poor conditions as compared to most American standards. Only 10% or 17.8 million are *double orphans*; children who have lost both parents. Even some of this 10% live with extended family. According to one report, 80% of children in orphanages still have families. Families frequently use orphanages as boarding schools when they find it difficult to support the children but do not necessarily want to give their children up to adoption (Joyce, 2013).

The numbers are misleading at best and the sad reality is that, not infrequently, children are adopted to US families and find later that they do have family back in their countries. Birth parents are misled into relinquishing their children thinking it is short term. Cultural understandings of adoption differ from country to country In the US we understand adoption to be a permanent, legal transaction, whereas in many countries it is thought to be temporary and a way for children to get an education and opportunities so they can come back to support their families. It is not thought of as a break in the first family bonds.

The final concern is colorblind mentality within the movement. Many international adoptions are transracial; therefore, adoptive families and communities need to understand racial identity, potential racial conflict, institutionalized racism, White privilege, White supremacy, and White fragility (Deangelo, 2018). This kind of training, reflection and emphasis seems sorely absent. According to one adoptee and adoption scholar, "There's a difference between celebrating diversity and understanding racism" (Kim, 2014).

Troubling Deception in Ethiopia

Adoption corruption most recently has been uncovered in Guatemala, Liberia, Haiti, Russia, Uganda and the Democratic Republic of Congo. In addition, the adoption practices and abuses in Ethiopia are a good case study and one of the saddest and most widespread examples of adoption gone wrong (Joyce, 2013; noWhitesaviors.org).

Following the close of adoptions in Guatemala under the Ortega Law in 2008 due to widespread adoption fraud, the demand for orphans turned to Ethiopia. Between 2008 and 2017 Ethiopian adoptions flourished. But in 2017, the Ethiopian government declared that all intercountry adoptions would be suspended, and then totally banned all intercountry adoptions in January of 2018 (Montgomery & Powell, 2018).

Traditionally, adoption was thought of as a way for infertile people or single people to start a family. But within the Christian Adoption Movement, some evangelical people see adoption as a religious calling, and many seek to adopt multiple children from developing countries. This demand creates a robust market for adoptable children. In Ethiopia, this demand created perverse incentives to provide children (Davis, 2013). The pattern is that a great deal of money is available through adoptions to local people who become, essentially *child finders*. In some instances, pregnant women are paid to give up their babies, kidnappings occur, and families sell their children thinking they will get a better life and education in America. The Ethiopian parents in many cases didn't understand that adoption is forever; these concepts are foreign to Ethiopian culture. The cutting of family ties and parental rights that exist in America through adoption do not exist. Birthparents by placing their children in Ethiopian orphanages hoped their children would be well fed and educated. The result is that orphanages flourish many times with babies and children that are not true orphans, and more orphanages were established due to supply and demand just to be filled with Ethiopian babies for White parents. To be fair, it was not only the evangelical adoption movement that was responsible for this tragedy, there were other religious and secular actors and agencies as well (Graff, 2017). But clearly there were hidden structures of organized crime centered on adoption corruption, and fraud flourished. Overtime, the reputations of adoption agencies in Ethiopia were damaged even though some adoptions were probably legitimate and meeting a real orphan's need for a family.

The counter argument to this troubling story of Ethiopian deception and corruption is that adoption agencies cannot be held responsible for false information given to them by birth families, and that the Ethiopian debacle was just a case of a few bad apples. But unfortunately, the Ethiopian government determined corruption was widespread, so much so that it created a new profession of adoption searchers and private investigators to find out the back-stories of adoptive children. This new profession replaced the child finders, recruiters who were paid per child per adoption.

For the Ethiopians this tragedy was a matter of national pride and the loss of identity for their children (Peralta, 2018). This is not to say that there are not successful, and beautiful examples of Ethiopian adoptions such as the case of the Blaszak family who adopted a nine year girl—a real orphan living in destitution who after years of legal and emotional battles was brought to the US where she seems to be thriving. These exceptions must be protected and remembered within the larger tragedies in Ethiopia (WSLS 10 News, 2017).

Learning from Rwanda

The Christian movement pledges to bring the "end of orphans in the world" but unfortunately adoption does not get to the root causes that create orphans—poverty and structural insecurities within countries. Lessons learned from Guatemala and Ethiopia are helping both the evangelical movement, governments and adoption agencies to move more cautiously and holistically in Rwanda. Rwanda is keeping the necessary paper trails, making real efforts to identify true orphans and slowing down the entire process and number of adoptions to make sure that they are legitimate and in the best interests of the child.

Rwandans also realize that adoption is not the only way to do orphan care. There must be a holistic solution including supporting orphanages and programs to aid poverty-stricken families to raise their own children (Stetzer, 2013). Christian activists and evangelical missionaries from the US seem now to be partnering to make adoption extremely difficult but healthier with less fraud by evaluating each adoption more carefully. Also, these partners are supporting alternative programs that assist families in keeping their children through healthcare initiatives and recruiting Rwandan families to do foster care and take care of vulnerable children within their own community. Saddleback Church in Rwanda is one good example of this outreach which provides healthcare, clean water, preschool, and other anti-poverty initiatives. There are lessons from the Rwandan approach (Davis, 2018). According to one church adoption leader, Christians should:

Keep adopting. Be careful and discerning. Only work with reputable agencies. But don't let Joyce's misinformation, and a willing media ready to spread that misinformation, keep you from loving that child sitting alone in an orphanage without hope . . . . Adoption has the potential to drastically change an orphan's life forever, but due diligence is needed (Stetzer, 2013).

And in the words of Medefind,

Is it possible that the Christian orphan care movement carries both strengths and weaknesses like many other important movements: prone to certain excesses and enthusiasms, at times naïve, always needing of improvement and self-correction—and yet ultimately effecting deep and lasting good for millions? . . . Only time will tell" (Associated Press, 2013).

Rebecca

I want to adopt. I want to give someone the same experience I had. Kids need love and a family. I think it is selfish to say you want children, but you don't want to adopt. I think that is selfish. Adoption is better than leaving a child abandoned.

I was really struck by one lady who wanted a child so badly and came to Haiti to adopt. Soon after she got pregnant and didn't want to tell the orphanage because she thought they wouldn't want her to have the child. She asked Elsie "Can you bring the child to me? So, the child was brought to the hospital in America where the woman was giving birth. She told Elsie, "I really still wanted to adopt. I felt embarrassed." Elsie said, "No, this situation just makes me think more that you want to have this child." That's a very beautiful thing.

Adoption is a poignant, beautiful, life changing experience. There are enough examples and history including the narratives in this book to testify to this fact. Adoption can be God driven, authentic—a miracle of sorts; we know this to be true. It is indeed as authentic and powerful as any parent-child relationship by birth, perhaps more so.

Joni

We could have had more children by birth. It was not that we were infertile. We wanted to adopt. We wanted you. We chose you. I can't imagine adopting a child then finding out that the child was either taken from her parents under false assumptions or just plain kidnapped. That would be devastating and heartbreaking.

Figure 10.2   *Growing up with brothers*

I never heard of this movement until we wrote this book. That this big push for adoption could be going on in the Evangelical Church was news to me. We adopted you in 1990 before any of this. I certainly don't have first-hand experience with individuals in the movement but what seems disturbing is the emphasis on the saving and rescuing of children, and not about the long-lasting love of the relationship and the culture, background and identity of the children.

I tried to make your birthmother invisible. But I don't think I want that anymore. We will probably never know who she was or is—however, I feel like I know her through you. And I want to tell her that she has a beautiful, smart, accomplished, sensitive daughter who is my daughter, too. I guess I wanted to erase her because I wanted to be your mother so badly. But that has happened, and I am grateful that she gave birth to you. I can only imagine that she was a beautiful woman, strong—I imagine she had a gap. They told us at the orphanage that you were abandoned at the hospital and that your birth mother died in childbirth. You were at the orphanage from the time you were an infant. On your birth certificate was the mayor of Port-au-Prince's name. You were a ward of the state, "loaned" to the orphanage. This is all we were told. It was required at the time in 1989 that a notice be put out in the local newspapers to see if any family members claimed you; no one responded. We were reasonably sure that you had no living birth family. But someone special conceived you and gave you birth—I know that because you are so special. I am grateful for this. I have no problem loving more than one child—so my daughter can conceivably love more than one mother. This acknowledgment doesn't make me the second mother, or second place. I will always be Mom, Mommy, and Mother.

Coda

Rebecca and Joni

Madeleine L'Engle says that to write a story is an incarnational activity, and the artists (writers) are birth-givers. Like Mary being obedient to bear the Child, the storytellers are obedient to tell their stories (2001). We have tried to be obedient. To us, adoption is a mystery and an event that was "done unto us." It is painful sometimes to do the research on the history and policies of adoption and to understand the muddy, complicated, sometimes unethical, damaging, and yes, sometimes mystical elements of adoption especially as it surrounds people of faith and the church.

We do not view the aligning of Christianity and adoption as necessarily negative. For us adoption was an answered prayer, a call from God, a mystery of faith. But we also don't want to stick our heads in the sand and not recognize that the adoption system is sometimes ugly, unethical, misdirected, racist, and tragically uniformed at best. As the late Rachel Held Evans (2012) said, "If Christians have learned anything from our rocky two-thousand-year theological history, it is that we make the most beautiful things ugly when we try to systematize mystery" (p. 114). This relationship between God, faith, and adoption is as all truth, all beauty, complicated, contextual, specific yet generalized. It is our story for sure. It is our adventure and paradox.

References

Associated Press. (November 23, 2015). Christian evangelical adoption movement perseveres amid criticism, drop in foreign adoptions. Fox News.

Bell, D. (1980). Brown v. Board of Education and the interest-convergence dilemma. *Harvard Law Review* 93(3), pp. 518–533.

Christian Alliance for Orphans, https://cafo.org/summit/. Accessed January 12, 2020.

Crary, D. (October 28, 2013). *Evangelical adoption movements faces criticism.* The Christian Science Monitor.

Davenport, D. (05/01/2010). What's in a Name? Birth Mother? First Mother? Real Mother? Creating a Family https://creatingafamily.org/adoption-category/whats-birth-mother-mother/

Davis, D. (April 15, 2013). How Evangelical Christians are Preaching the New Gospel of Adoption. Interview: Kathryn Joyce, the author of 'The Child Catchers.' Fresh Air. Philadelphia: National Public Radio.

Diangelo, R. (2018). *White fragility: Why it is so hard for White people to talk about racism.* Boston: Beacon Press.

Ellison, M. (2003). Authoritative knowledge and single women's unintentional pregnancies, abortions, adoption and single motherhood: Social stigma and structural violence. *Medical Anthropology Quarterly,* 17(3), 322–347.

Graff, E. J. (May 3, 2017). They steal babies, don't they? *Pacific Standard.* https://psmag.com/news/they-steal-babies-dont-they-international-adoption-schuster-institute-95027. Accessed January 2, 2020.

Held-Evans, R. (2012). *A year of Biblical womanhood.* Nashville: Thomas Nelson.

Herman, Ellen (2012) The Adoption History Project. https://pages.uoregon.edu/adoption/people/holt.htm

Joyce, K. (2013). *The child catchers: Rescue, trafficking, and the new gospel of adoption.* New York: Public Affairs.

Kim. (December 22, 2014). How adoption has forced evangelicals to grapple with race relations. Religion News Service author Bailey, S. P. https://religionnews.com/2014/12//22/adoption-forced-evangelicals-grapple-race-relations/

L'Engle, M. (2001). *Walking on water: Reflections on faith and art.* New York: Convergent Books.

Montgomery, M. & Powell, I. (March 1, 2018). International adoptions have dropped 72% since 2005—here's why. The Conversation. http://theconversation.com/international-adoptions-have-dropped-72-%-since2005-heres-why-91809

Musingsofabirthmom.com/2014/07/15/baby-scoop-era-vs-coercion-era/ Baby Scoop Era Vs. Coercion Era.

National Indian Law Library, Welcome to the online edition of "A Practical Guide to the Indian Child Welfare Act" https://www.narf.org/nill/documents/icwa/index.html

Peralta, E. (April 2, 2018). In Ethiopia, a new ban on foreign adoptions is about national pride. *Newscast.* New York: National Public Radio.

Petrie, A. (1998). *Gone to aunt's: Remembering Canada's home for unwed mothers.* Toronto: McClelland & Stewart.

Stetzer, E. (April 19, 2013) Christianity Today—Evangelicals and Adoption: An Evil Obsession? https://www.chirstianitytoday.com/edstetzer/2013/april/evangelicals-and-adoption-evil-obsession.html

WSLS 10 News, (2017). The long journey home. https://www.youtube.com/watch?v=8p3COZW9_DE

EPILOGUE

We are in Rebecca's Brooklyn apartment reading through the final manuscript of this book before sending it to the publisher. Rebecca returned to the US with a longing for more stability. She wanted to settle down in one place to focus on other desires such as finding a spouse and starting a family, among other things. Joni lives several miles away in Brooklyn too; two adult women who have come full circle in our relationship. We read this manuscript editing, deleting, while laughing and plotting our next life and writing adventures for surely "His favor lasts a lifetime." (Psalm 30:5, New International Version) Having discovered different parts of ourselves, there are still many unknowns for both of us; we didn't think this is how life would be. Rebecca keeps pouring the sweet wine.

Rebecca's apartment is homey with scented candles, lots of light, and a few artifacts from her childhood; we both love to nest. Space matters and we both inhabit, decorate, and try to make our spaces beautiful. We are alike in this way creating home wherever we live for however long. Spreading the pages of this manuscript on the sofa and the floor, we tread our way chapter by chapter talking through our writing adventure.

We did not begin writing a book about race but one about our relationship. But the story could not be told without it. Rebecca wants to know more of her mother's exploration of race as so much of the book she says is about her exploration. We both have come to the same conclusion that we have privilege of different types and that with privilege comes responsibility. We conclude that we are responsible to speak our truths about race and act in ways that show how it matters very much, but in many ways does not matter at all—within our mother and daughter love relationship. This book is one attempt.

Books are occupants of our spaces both externally and internally. We love reading, even as children we both did. There is something about the feel of a book, the engagement in someone else's story and the connections it makes to our own lives. As Dinaw Mengestu (2007) says in his poignant book, *The Beautiful Things that Heaven Bears*, "I've kept a book close at hand so that every hour of even the quietest days has been filled with at least one voice other than my own." For us the other voice has been that of history; our companion voice throughout this book.

On another evening we are reading through the first draft of this epilogue, at a cozy restaurant on 57th St and 9th Avenue in Manhattan, so much of our writing is over a meal; Rebecca says we need to include the theme of time. Our times together, how time shaped us, how we have sat, thought, lived in the present moments, not wasting time. We try not to kill time but to inhabit it.

We hope we have not taken ourselves too seriously. This evening we certainly laugh at ourselves and our stories, "It is the heart that's not yet sure of its God that is afraid to laugh in His presence" (MacDonald, 1879). Indeed we must laugh because this book contains so much that is not humorous. In the Bible, Ephesians 6:10 calls out the "spiritual forces of evil in the heavenly realms" (New International Version), which we identify as historical institutionalized racism, in some cases, as it relates to the adoption of children. These are not easy stories to tell.

After an evening at Rebecca's home enjoying a dinner of salad, salmon, capers, and olives over a bed of spinach, Joni leaves with the sweet wine on her lips, the manuscript in hand, and a slight high from the evening of thinking and talking and feeling. We think that if we had had the choice, we would have picked each other for mother and daughter from the start.

Rebecca walks Joni to the Uber and makes sure the driver is legitimate and tells Joni to call when she arrives home safely. The manuscript will be submitted in a few days and then the story will no longer be just ours. This disclosing is a bit scary but also sweet like the wine we shared this evening.

References

MacDonald, G. (1879). *Sir Gibbie: A novel.* Philadelphia, PA: J. B. Lippincott.

Mengestu, D. (2007). *The beautiful things that heaven bears.* New York: Penguin Group.

The Holy Bible, New International Version. (1984). Grand Rapids: Zondervan Publishing House.

INDEX

www.ingramcontent.com/pod-product-compliance
Lightning Source LLC
Chambersburg PA
CBHW050607280326
41932CB00016B/2944

"Binfet and Tardif-Williams have written an exceptional book that delves into the rapid growth and changes in animal-assisted interventions, particularly focusing on preserving the welfare of therapy dog teams. It emphasizes the crucial importance of supporting good welfare practices for therapy animals. These practices not only benefit the animals themselves but also directly impact the well-being of the participants, the team, and the efficacy of the treatment. The authors present a wealth of practical and insightful suggestions, all firmly rooted in empirical evidence and best practices in the field. This book offers a comprehensive overview of canine-assisted interventions (CAI), significantly enhancing readers' understanding of the subject. The volume is easy to read and provides interesting scenarios and case studies. I wholeheartedly endorse this book for students and professionals interested in practising and researching animal-assisted interventions. This resource will enhance the readers' competencies in CAI and provide immediate, practical guidance for anyone working with therapy animals."

Aubrey Fine, PhD, *professor emeritus, Cal Poly State University, Pomona; adjunct professor, Utah State University, Logan; licensed psychologist, author, and speaker*

"This book is a must-read for those seeking to elevate the standards of canine-assisted interventions. Binfet and Tardif-Williams expertly navigate the complexities of optimizing outcomes for both humans and animals in various therapeutic settings. By masterfully blending research insights with practical applications, the authors provide a roadmap for maximizing therapeutic benefits across diverse settings. Their insights and practical recommendations make this an essential resource for researchers, practitioners, and anyone passionate about enhancing the well-being of therapy dogs and their handlers."

Lori Kogan, PhD, *editor in chief, Human-Animal Interactions; professor, College of Veterinary Medicine and Biomedical Sciences, Colorado State University*

"This is a comprehensive, much-needed guide that seamlessly translates research into safe and effective practice of canine-assisted interventions for various populations, settings, and contexts. Emphasizing why and how to optimize the dog-handler relationship, Drs. Binfet and Tardif-Williams provide essential tools and examples to safeguard animal welfare while facilitating positive intervention effects."

Patricia Pendry, PhD, *professor, Washington State University*

"Professors Binfet and Tardif-Williams draw from their decades of experience where they have provided people interactions with companion animals in a variety of contexts. Realizing that the welfare of the therapy dog-handler team is centrally important in shaping the outcomes of the interactions, they draw from extensive research to explain the complex factors involved in ensuring dog and handler welfare. Now having strong professional leadership, the field of companion animal interactions can use this book to incorporate the emerging research-based knowledge on criteria for considering animal and human welfare in all current contexts where these interactions are used."

Lynette Hart, PhD, professor emeritus, University
of California Davis School of Veterinary Medicine

"This book is a timely contribution to the rapidly evolving field of canine-assisted interventions. Drs. Binfet and Tardif-Williams achieved their goal of raising awareness and sparking discussion about the crucial need to safeguard and enhance the welfare of therapy dog-handler teams in both practice and research. The evidence-based, real-life scenarios and thought-provoking questions are an important resource for anyone interested in advancing the field to ensure the well-being of therapy dogs, handlers, and participants alike."

Colleen Dell, PhD, professor and Centennial Enhancement
Chair in One Health and Wellness, Department of Sociology, University of Saskatchewan